# Gypsy Bride

# Gypsy Bride

One girl's true story of
falling in love with a gypsy boy

## Sam Skye Lee

EBURY
PRESS

1 3 5 7 9 10 8 6 4 2

Published in 2011 by Ebury Press, an imprint of Ebury Publishing
A Random House Group company

The Random House Group Limited Reg. No. 954009

Addresses for companies within the Random House Group can be found
at www.randomhouse.co.uk

A CIP catalogue record for this book is available from the British Library

The Random House Group Limited supports the Forest Stewardship
Council® (FSC®), the leading international forest certification
organisation. All our titles that are printed on Greenpeace approved
FSC® certified paper carry the FSC® logo. Our paper procurement policy
can be found at www.randomhouse.co.uk/environment.

Designed and set by seagulls.net

Printed in the UK by CPI Cox & Wyman, Reading, RG1 8EX

ISBN 9780091944896

To buy books by your favourite authors and register for offers visit
www.randomhouse.co.uk

*In memory of Martin Norton (1983 – 2011).*
*Always missed, never forgotten.*

# Prologue

'Where's my husband?'

It was the first time that I had said the 'H' word in relation to myself and at first it felt alien in my mouth.

I rolled it around on my tongue again.

'Husband,' I repeated quietly under my breath. A faint smile flitted across my lips, like one of the delicate crystal-encrusted butterflies sown carefully on to my dress. I was a married woman at last and, although it had only been an hour or so since I'd said my vows, I felt a sense of peace and belonging that, now I had found it, I didn't even know had been missing from my life. Even after such a short period of time, being a wife already seemed to suit me. It was meant to be.

I was now Mrs Samantha Skye Lee, newlywed. But at that particular moment I was missing the most important man in my life, my new hubby Patrick. We'd been together just a few minutes ago but he'd disappeared just as one of the most important parts of the day was approaching. For months I had kept what I was about to show him a secret and I wanted Pat to be bowled over when I revealed it.

I was squirming with anticipation. 'Where is he?' I asked his mum Karen urgently.

She shrugged and hurried off to find him while I crept into a side room to prepare with the only people in the room who knew my secret – Thelma the dressmaker and her two assistants.

I looked through a small window in the door at the room outside. It was full of loved ones: my family and friends, my new family, and the exotic cast of characters that had welcomed me into their strange community. I was 17 years old, my future was stretching out before me, and I knew that I would be walking towards it arm in arm with Pat.

The room was a whirl of activity and excitement but at that moment time seemed to slow down. I had been told that wedding days are so hectic and so emotional, they often pass in a blur with only one or two moments of clarity where you get the opportunity to take in everything and appreciate what is happening around you. You wake up a bundle of nerves in the morning and somehow, before you know it, you are standing in a half-empty hall or pub, it is dark outside, most of the guests have gone home and the day is over. By that standard my day had been the same as many others. I couldn't believe that half the day had already gone. It had started with a family row and had progressed to a frantic race to reach the church on time. Getting to the altar had been no easy feat, and after the ceremony we had caused a traffic jam of over 100 cars on the way to the venue, thanks mainly to one aspect of my big day: my dress. With 105 rings of fabric puffing it out to over eight feet in diameter, the dress literally stopped traffic. And the glass carriage we travelled in allowed everyone to see it. But that wasn't even the real showstopper. I had yet to reveal the ace up my jewel-encrusted satin sleeve and before that happened I wanted to make the most of the lull in proceedings and drink in my surroundings.

I breathed deeply, consciously trying to still my racing mind. We were in a social club in St Helens, between Manchester and Liverpool. Behind the dance floor the karaoke screen was switched on and waiting for the first brave guest to start warbling away. The DJ had set up his decks and the lights on his mobile rig were flicking in coloured sequence.

Over in a corner there was my mum Linda, her blond hair almost white against her dusky pink-and-black outfit, and my dad Brian, his eyes twinkling with pride. Mum and Dad had separated when I was little but got on well. Dad was at the wedding with his partner Jamie; they had been together since I was five and had been engaged for many years but never married. Bouncing around excitedly were their children, my younger half sister and mini-me bride Tiffany with her brother Morgan. My older brothers Dean and Brian were enjoying a drink and chatting at the bar. Then there was my new family: Pat's mum Karen, his sister Chantelle and brothers Levi and John Thomas. I took a moment to reflect. It wasn't just a special day because I was getting married. It was special because two cultures were coming together.

To all intents and purposes I was what most people would call a normal girl. I had grown up as part of a normal working-class family in a normal semi-detached house in a normal part of north-west England. But one part of my life was, to outsiders at least, distinctly abnormal. I had fallen deeply in love with a traveller. For two years I had been courted by a gypsy boy and had integrated into his community. I had learned about traveller customs and traditions and now I was marrying into his way of life. When the day was over I would move out of my mum's house and go to live in the trailer that Pat had bought for us on the site where his family lived.

But before any of that could happen I needed to reveal my secret.

The buzz of voices in the room outside started to die down and the guests were ushered to the edge of the dance floor as the lights were dimmed. It was a riot of colours and exotic outfits. My bridesmaids in black and pink were smiling and mouthing the words *good luck* to me as I walked out into the darkness. People clapped, others gasped. And then, in the corner of my eye, I saw a flash of white walk through the door. Pat.

The crowd parted to let him through and our eyes met.

'It's our first dance, babe,' I said gently, but he didn't seem to hear me. He was too distracted, looking me up and down, drinking me in. My dress had revealed its final secret.

Sewn expertly into the fabric were hundreds of lights which twinkled like stars in the night sky, illuminating the billowing fabric like the Milky Way. And nestled in the folds of chiffon and satin the butterflies had begun to flutter their robotic wings and dance their hypnotic dance.

My dress had come alive.

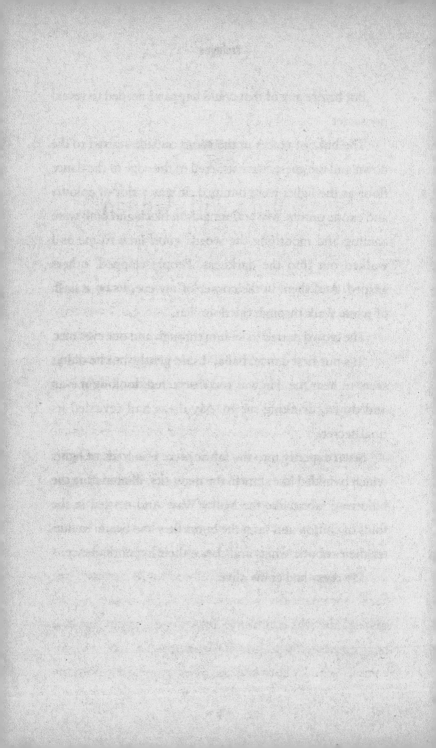

# 1

# Accidents Will Happen

My first memory was of blood. There was plenty of it. It filled my mouth and trickled down my throat. I was only around four years old and although I can't remember the pain, I must have been hurt badly because I was screaming so much that the window I had been looking out of was covered in a fine red mist of spray.

I remember my older brother Brian too. He was standing next to me with a look on his face that was sheepish and terror-struck in equal measure. He did what most little boys do when they realise they are in trouble; he skulked away with a look on his face that clearly said *oops!* As he shuffled off, Mum, alerted by the noise, ran into the room to see what the commotion was about. Her hand automatically went to her open mouth as she gasped. She was confronted by a scene straight out of a horror movie, with me looking exactly like a mini-vampire who had just enjoyed a hearty meal. By now, the blood was dripping off my chin and spreading a crimson stain across my clean white top.

I had been the victim of a prank that went wrong. I didn't know it then but it was something I would have to get used to over the following years. In this instance I had decided to climb on to a chair pulled up to my bedroom window so I could look outside. I had hoisted myself up to the windowsill with my chubby arms so I could see into the garden and watch the biggest member of our family – Vinnie the horse – as he ate the grass in our backyard. Every so often he would come and stay for the day, and having him there was always a novelty.

We were lucky enough to have a big area at the rear of the house for him and there weren't many houses that I knew of which had horses in the back garden, so for an inquisitive tot like me, the curiosity was just too much. I loved Vinnie and nothing was going to stop me from seeing him now that he'd come to visit from the stables where he usually lived, not even the fact that I was too small to see out of the window.

Brian, who at six was two years older than me, had walked past my open bedroom door and seen me standing there on the chair. It was an opportunity too good to miss, and as I gazed through the glass in awe of the giant creature grazing on the lawn outside, he crept up behind me and pulled my legs away. My arms buckled and I dropped like a stone, catching my chin on the windowsill. *Crunch*! I almost bit clean through my lip.

It took weeks for the nasty injury to heal, during which time people would stare at me as I walked down the street with Mum, my fat lip red, swollen and disfigured. It didn't help the healing process when, a few weeks after the incident, my other older brother Dean, who is five years older than me, tripped me up as I ran past him. I fell flat on my face and split open the wound for a second time.

Mum and Dad soon got used to patching me up and I quickly learnt that if I was to survive, I needed to toughen up. The lip was just the start. Another time, I was sitting in the family car waiting for Mum to drop a DVD back to the local Blockbuster store. I was strapped in my seat in the back and Brian was in the front in the passenger's seat. I watched him fiddle around with something in the centre console and heard a click.

We had been told repeatedly not to touch anything in the car.

'You're not allowed to play with that,' I scolded, ever the annoying little sister.

Brian turned around and I caught sight of something red and glowing in his hand. He had the mischievous look on his face that meant that trouble wasn't far away.

'What's tha—' I began to ask. Before I got a chance to finish the sentence a searing hot pain flashed up my leg and strangled my words. The object Brian had been playing with was the car's cigarette lighter and he had pushed it into the soft flesh of my leg like a cowboy branding a cow. When Mum came back the car was full of my screams and the smell of burnt flesh. To this day I still have the scars from my brother's prank. Mum and Dad would always stick up for me. They were protective of me because I was the only girl.

Life as the only girl in the house could be tricky. Often I was stuck between the urge to have fun with my older brothers and the knowledge that if I did, I would be playing with fire – sometimes literally as in the case of the cigarette lighter. On one occasion we were in the kitchen helping with the food and one of my brothers was hogging the rolling pin. I wanted a go with it too and tried to yank it out of his hands. As I tugged at it he threw a freshly cooked pizza in my face like a comedy custard pie. As Mum peeled the melted cheese off me, skin came off with it.

And then there was the first Christmas I can remember. It was spent in hospital and once again Dean had something to do with that.

It was Christmas Eve, and like all children I was so excited I felt like I was about to burst. However, as I suffered from bad asthma at times, especially during the winter, Mum and Dad were determined to try and keep me calm. Anxiety and excitement triggered the condition and I had suffered a few severe attacks. Despite the dangers of making me hyper, Dean decided to wind me up.

'Santa's coming, Sam,' he whispered as we were getting ready for bed. 'Can't you hear his sleigh? He's coming with all the presents.'

'Where is he?' I gasped as I began to jump up and down uncontrollably.

'He's on the roof, Sam, we're going to see him any second now,' Dean continued.

It was at that point that I started to feel my chest tighten. As I continued to jump up and down my breaths began to come in shorter and shorter gasps and my heart started to race. Soon I was feeling light-headed. My legs were getting weaker and I needed to sit down.

Even at that age I recognised the signs and realised that I was having an asthma attack, but this only made matters worse, because I believed Santa was about to make an entrance with a sack full of toys and that I was going to pass out and miss him. I got myself increasingly worked up, using the diminishing breaths in my tiny lungs to gasp the word *Santa* over and over. When I went blue, Dean called my parents.

I was rushed to A&E where I was put on a nebuliser and given steroid inhalers and oxygen to stabilise my airways. I remember waking up groggily on Christmas Day in the children's ward at Billinge Hospital. My family were at my bedside looking drained. Noel Edmonds was on the TV with his *Christmas Presents* programme and was visiting children in hospital to take them gifts. I kept wondering if he was going to turn up on my ward.

There was one advantage of being in hospital on Christmas Day, though. Eventually I did get to see Santa. He came to visit us after we had our Christmas dinner. I could see the blue of his doctor's uniform underneath the costume, and he sounded very much like the doctor who had examined my chest that morning, but it didn't matter. As far as I was concerned he was the real deal and he even bought us poorly children presents.

Billinge Hospital was already familiar to my mum and dad because, on a bright spring day in 1993, it was where Mum went to give birth to me. It has long since closed down, and has been redeveloped into a housing estate, and I find it strange to think of people going about their daily lives in the place where I, and many other children, were born. By all accounts I was a happy, chubby baby with a shock of dark hair, dark eyes and chubby little hands that loved to explore. I was named Samantha Skye

Norton and I was part of a family that included Brian and Dean and my half-brother Carl who was 11 years older than me and who Mum had before she met my dad and who lived with my maternal grandparents. He had been settled with them when Dad met Mum and decided to stay there, rather than move to a new house.

Home for me was Edward Street in Haydock, a former coal-mining town near St Helens in Merseyside, which is almost halfway between Liverpool and Manchester and famous for its racecourse. We lived in a comfortable three-bedroom, semi-detached house in a quiet street. We had the luxury of a big back garden with a lush lawn, big enough for those times that Vinnie came over to stay.

Mum didn't work when I was younger but Dad ran his own haulage firm and although we were not rich, we didn't want for much. Mum was a precursor of today's yummy mummy; she loved dressing up and wore trendy, revealing outfits. She would regularly pop off for sunbed sessions and would come home looking like she had spent a week in the Caribbean, rather than an afternoon in St Helens.

We were a normal family and did the things normal families do. A treat was a trip to the cinema or McDonald's and we'd have days out at the seaside or the park. Sometimes we'd head off to North Wales where we'd stay in a caravan or a chalet, and we took holidays abroad to places such as the Canary Islands and Spain.

So even though I often ended up the brunt of one of my brother's pranks, there was still a lot of love in our household. In those early years I don't remember any rows between Mum and Dad. The only bickering in the house was between me, Dean and Brian. In many ways, we had an idyllic life.

We were also a family of animal lovers and as far back as I can remember there were always pets in and around the home to look after. We lived in a suburban street but we may as well have been on a farm. We had dogs and rabbits and a host of other pets, which I adored. I learned how to care for things when I was young and despite the odd mishap, such as when I forgot to feed my pet rabbit over the Christmas week because of all the excitement, I became a proper little Dr Doolittle. I chatted away to our pet boxer dog Charlie and when I was just a few years old, Vinnie became part of our family too. Within days we were best friends and I would tell him all my secrets.

Mum had grown up with horses. She had one when she was a little girl and continued to love them through her life. As many girls before me have discovered, once you have a horse you are hooked for life and Mum was definitely hooked on Vinnie.

She bought him when I was four and he was a giant of a horse, a cross between a shire horse and a thoroughbred. He was 18-and-a-half hands high, a far cry from the dainty ponies that most little girls start out riding on. He was light brown with huge shoulders and haunches and as a four-year-old, I could feel the earth shake when he clip-clopped towards me on the farm where he was usually kept. He had a white flash down his nose and the deepest, kindest eyes I have ever seen on an animal. When I talked to him I felt he understood what I was telling him.

Mum was fixated with Vinnie too and twice a day she would go to feed, groom and ride him. Whenever I could I would go with her. It was the highlight of my day.

I sat on Vinnie for the first time some time after we got him and from the vantage point high on his back I swear I could see for miles and miles. It was exhilarating and a little bit scary but I knew Vinnie would never do anything to harm me and even if he did, having two boisterous brothers ensured that I had quickly toughened up. After having sizzling pizza thrown in my face and cigarette lighters held to my legs, there wasn't much that scared me.

As well as making me braver than perhaps was good for me, being a little girl in a male-dominated household affected me another way: I was a tomboy.

In Edward Street there weren't any other girls my age to play with so inevitably I spent my younger years trailing around behind my brothers. As a toddler they were not interested in allowing me to play their games but as I became older they realised that I was not going to go away and that if they wanted some peace and quiet from my constant pestering, they would have to include me.

Begrudgingly they began to accept me into their boys' world. We would play super heroes, cops and robbers and other rough-and-tumble games. Most of the time I would come out worse off, but through my tears I would secretly be glad that they had let me play.

While other girls my age were getting acquainted with Barbie dolls and Tinkerbelle, I was playing with Action Men. The Disney Princess craze passed me by, which is surprising when you think about my fairy-tale wedding. I didn't know Pocahontas from Princess Jasmine but I did know how to climb a tree and how to pop a wheelie on a bike.

I'm sure Mum was horrified to see the type of girl I was growing into. My wardrobe looked more like a boy's, with the pretty dresses she bought me stuffed messily at the back. I hated pink, I hated bows and I hated most girlie things. The only concession I made to my mum's need to dress me up was my hair. My mum could control the way it was cut and made sure it was long and flowing.

Mum was forever trying to persuade me to dress like a normal little girl but she was fighting a losing battle. 'Please, Sam,' she'd beg as we got ready for one family function or another, 'just put on that lovely pink dress I got you last week. You'll look like a beautiful princess.'

'Yuck,' I'd reply, pulling on a pair of tracksuit bottoms. In baggy jeans and trainers I'd zoom off on my bike with my brothers for another adventure.

Even my musical tastes were distinctly un-girlie. While my contemporaries were dreaming of being like their idols, the Spice Girls, my favourite song during my early years was 'Witch Doctor' by the Cartoons. I loved the nonsensical chorus of made-up words and would bound around my bedroom repeating it over and over.

All that energy had to go somewhere and, thanks to my brothers and the fact that we lived in an area surrounded by a high concentration of Premiership football clubs, I soon started kicking a ball around and discovered I had a natural talent for the game. Later, when I started school, I began playing in a team. The funny thing was that I hated watching football on TV and I didn't know any players. They could have passed me on the street and I wouldn't have recognised them. Some of them probably did, as many of the big teams stayed in the posh hotel just up the road from our house before games.

All things considered, life in Edward Street in those first years of my life was cosy and happy. Despite the frequent brother-initiated dramas I was safe, secure and loved.

And to be fair on them, it wasn't always my brothers that landed me in trouble. I developed a sense of inquisitiveness which, years later, would help to change the course of my life and lead me to meet the man of my dreams. As a toddler, however, it almost always resulted in some form of medical drama. Like the time I almost poisoned myself.

It was a hot summer afternoon and I had been playing in the garden with Brian and Dean. Vinnie was back at the stables so we had the lawn to ourselves and had made a tent from an old sheet and a couple of garden chairs, under which we had been sheltering for shade. While Brian and Dean guarded our new camp I ran inside the house to get a drink.

'Mum, I'm thirsty,' I yelled. 'Can I get a drink of something?'

Mum was on the telephone to one of her friends. I could hear her nattering away in the lounge and walked in to get her attention. I mimed raising a glass to my lips so she knew what I was asking and she held her hand over the mouthpiece and gestured to the kitchen.

'I've just been shopping. There are bottles of pop on the kitchen counter,' she explained. 'Help yourself but don't drink too much, you're having your tea soon.'

I wandered into the kitchen and looked up at the bottles lined up on the work surface ready to be put away in the fridge. There were bottles of Diet Coke, Fanta, Lemonade and Sunny Delight but I didn't fancy any of them. *Maybe there is something else behind them*, I thought to myself and dragged a stool up to the counter so I could climb up and have a better look at what was on offer.

I clambered up and rifled through the carrier bags until a bottle of clear liquid behind all the shopping caught my eye. It was an unmarked bottle and the sunlight from the kitchen window glinted through it invitingly. It looked to me like the mineral water that my mum liked to drink and exactly what I needed to quench my thirst. I unscrewed the blue plastic top and without hesitating raised the bottle to my lips and tipped my head back. I took several long, deep mouthfuls. At first nothing registered and so I drained the lot. It wasn't the sweet taste I had been expecting. Seconds later I felt a violent belch of gas escape from my stomach and rise up through my throat. It stung as I exhaled through my nose and my eyes started to water.

*What had I done?* I panicked. Another rumble erupted from my stomach and I started to feel dizzy.

I ran into the lounge and started to cry.

'I don't feel very well,' I sobbed to Mum, waving the empty bottle in front of her face. She grabbed it, sniffed it, and immediately hung up the phone.

I had no idea what I had just swallowed but I knew by the look on Mum's face that whatever it was would not be doing my insides any good.

'Oh my God,' she gasped. 'You've drunk a bottle of turps.'

Dad had been doing some painting around the house and the turps had been left safely out of reach for when he needed it to wash the paintbrushes. Neither Mum nor Dad had thought that I would fancy it as a cooling drink.

Mum sprang into action while I continued to belch out hot chemicals from my stomach. She grabbed my hand and led me over the road to one of our neighbours, who I think was a nurse or a pharmacist. Everybody on the street used to seek medical advice from her, so she must have been an expert.

'She's drunk turps,' Mum blurted out. 'What should I do?'

Calmly the neighbour explained that the worst thing I could do was try to be sick and bring the liquid up. She seemed to be an expert because she explained that turps comes from pine trees and although unpleasant probably would not kill me. That was a relief! She advised that the best thing I could do was to drink orange juice to neutralise the harmful effects the liquid may be having on my innards.

We ran back indoors and Mum got me a glass of orange juice, which I gulped down in a panic. She watched me like a hawk for the rest of the afternoon and the orange juice seemed to work because after a few hours my churning tummy settled and by the early evening I was back under our makeshift tent, impressing Brian and Dean with the story of how I had swallowed a whole bottle of poison, stared death in the face and survived.

They would never admit it of course but I knew by the way they listened quietly to my tale that they were impressed. If only for that evening I was no longer their annoying little sister. I was their equal – we were brothers in arms, even if every now and then Mum forced me to wear a dress. Life was perfect. Battle-hardened and invincible it seemed that nothing could come along and shatter our cosy little domestic bubble.

# 2

# Broken

My little ears strained to hear what they were saying, but the words were drowned out by the noise of passing cars and by Brian and Dean who were shouting at each other. I couldn't follow the thread of the conversation but I knew that what was being said was important.

I was four and us kids had been ushered outside. It was a warm spring afternoon and the sun was shining. Something was happening between Mum and Dad in the lounge and their voices were getting louder, more urgent. I couldn't quite hear them fully but I could tell by the tone something bad was taking place. I tried to work out what they were saying to each other.

'Shut up you two,' I hissed at my brothers as I tried to listen.

Call it a girl's intuition but I knew whatever Mum and Dad were talking about was serious. Like all kids faced with a domestic drama my first reaction was a sense of guilt. Had I done something wrong? Were they angry with me?

I kept looking through the front room window anyway, and every so often would see either Mum or Dad stride purposefully from one end of the room to the other, waving their arms, gesticulating wildly and pointing at each other.

My parents are both even-tempered people, and rows like this didn't happen in our household. A deep sense of unease was creeping into the pit of my stomach and I didn't like it. Outside on the street everything was the same as it always had been; same trees, same cars, same houses. But inside my home something was changing.

Random angry words, muffled by the windowpane, floated through the air. *Hurt, trust, leave.* I didn't understand what any of them meant but the tone and the way they were being delivered was full of hurt and bitterness.

To people passing we seemed like any normal children playing in the garden, the words from inside the house were too muffled to work out. Brian and Dean were largely oblivious. They were just thankful for the opportunity of a bit of free playtime out in the front garden. They only stopped their game and looked up when they heard the front door open.

Mum walked outside. She seemed crushed, as if something had been drained from her. Her face was creased with fury. Her normally perfect hair was tousled where she had been running her hands through it and her eyes were red and sad; she had been crying. I looked over to the window and saw Dad staring out. He looked suddenly old and defeated, his shoulders had drooped and when he saw me his gaze dropped. My little heart was beating hard in my chest. What was happening?

Mum slammed the door hard behind her and strode purposefully down the garden path towards me, sniffing back her tears as she approached.

'Come on, Sam,' she said. 'We need to go out.'

She told the boys to stay with my dad and strapped me into the car before gunning the engine and driving away. I didn't have a clue what had just happened but I remember looking out the car window as we drove off and seeing the house shrinking into the distance with my two brothers standing in the garden watching us go and my dad's shadow at the window.

'Where are we going, Mum?' I asked from the back seat. I could see my mum's eyes reflected in the rear-view mirror. They were puffy and bloodshot. She glanced back at me.

'We need to go away for a while,' she answered.

'Why?'

'Because there is no food in the fridge,' she said simply.

That was her explanation, clearly thought up on the spur of the moment and, as a totally trusting child, that's what I believed. We were leaving because there was not enough food in the house for us all to eat. No matter that we'd all had a decent breakfast a few hours earlier. Who was I to question my mum?

Of course, food shortages had nothing to do with it. Mum and Dad had decided to split up. It was over, and while Mum drove us off to stay with a friend for a while, Dad was in the process of moving out.

In the weeks that followed our lives changed beyond all recognition. Our new living arrangements were worked out and the hard negotiations of family breakdown preoccupied my parents. Even though they had never married, Mum had taken Dad's surname and there were financial and custody issues to be taken care of.

Much of this time is just a blurred memory to me. I know that Mum and I returned to the house in Edward Street and that Dad moved out and found a new house with Brian and Dean in a town five miles away called Blackbrook. The boys were asked who they wanted to stay with and were closer to Dad so chose to live mainly with him. As the weeks went by I started to notice things being taken out of the old family home. Spaces appeared where there had once been furniture as family possessions were divided up. Mum is and always has been a strong-willed woman and I can't ever remember her crumpling and falling apart during what must have been an immensely difficult time. Eventually the house was sold and we moved to a smaller house in nearby Norman Avenue.

The relationship between Mum and Dad was frosty in those early months. I would stay with Mum during the week and with Dad at the weekends. We would sometimes see each other during the week but I missed my daddy and even though life on my own with Mum was probably less hazardous, I missed my brothers as well. They would sometimes stay with Mum but mainly with Dad. We would see each other at weekends and, as the years went by, when we went on holidays. I would also see Brian at school but because he was a couple of years older than me he would be in a different part of the playground. It was hard at first to get used to our new living arrangements and I missed having someone to play with.

What I didn't understand at the time was that Mum and Dad were embroiled in a custody battle over me. They both wanted me to live with them. Because Brian and Dean were older, they had been given a choice, but my destiny would be decided by the court.

I was taken to a hearing where I was assessed by someone who I assume was a social worker. It was in a red-brick building that looked like a school and although it was a sunny day, all the radiators were on and the windows were shut. The whole place felt gloomy and oppressive and I was ushered into a room with faded children's posters on the walls and a plastic box of toys in the corner.

I was left to play for a while until a man in a brightly coloured tie and blue shirt with the sleeves rolled up walked in and smiled at me. He was carrying a thick pile of important-looking files and it was so warm in the room that he had dark sweat patches under his arms.

He sat down on one of the child-sized chairs and began to ask me questions. At first they were questions I was comfortable with: my name, my age, the names and ages of my brothers. He'd obviously read up about my family because he also asked me about Vinnie and my pets. But slowly the conversation turned to more personal matters. How was I feeling about what was going on at home? Was I happy with Mum, was I happy with Dad? And then came that one question which was hugely inappropriate to ask a four-year-old child.

'Who would you rather live with if you had the choice?'

Torn between loyalties to both parents I refused to answer. I felt that it was wrong to ask me that question and it was impossible for me to choose between Mum and

Dad – but I was only four and couldn't articulate what I was feeling. Even if I could I wouldn't tell this man. To his credit he did not pursue the matter and eventually it was decided that I would stay with Mum.

I am not the first person to come from a broken home and I certainly won't be the last. I sometimes wonder what effect that period had on me as I grew up. Perhaps I was lucky that it happened when I was so young. The memories I have of life before the split are happy on the whole. We did not go through years of arguments and traumas like some families do. When it happened, it happened quickly. Back then, of course I wanted Mum and Dad to stay together but with the benefit of hindsight their separation was a good thing. They both moved on with their lives and Dad now has other children with his partner Jamie so, if it wasn't for the split, I wouldn't have my half-sister Tiffany and my half-brother Morgan. My dad also has another daughter from a previous relationship – my half-sister Janet Louise, who I've never met but I would like to one day.

Later, I'd come to live in a community, a community that has stricter morals than the one I grew up in, but where concepts such as marriage, fidelity and the sanctity of the family unit is so strong that divorce is practically unheard of, and where children grow up surrounded by their brothers, sisters and cousins. The grown-up me would never have wanted my parents to stay together just for the children's sake, but separated from my brothers and the father that I loved so much, I was often lonely and a little bit sad. I didn't really think about it at the time, but it made me realise years later that what I wanted was a stable home life, and to raise my children in a loving, two-parent household.

The period of adjustment after the legal custody issues had been sorted out was difficult for everyone, and it took a long time to work through. Christmas was always particularly hard. We would alternate between Mum and Dad, staying with one parent overnight and in the morning one year, and the other overnight and in the morning the next. What this usually meant was that I would end up eating three Christmas dinners because in between the changeover, I would visit my grandparents who would also have a plate of food ready.

It was always hard leaving Mum alone or coming back to her after a morning with Dad because when I got back home I could see she had been crying. It was the only time the situation really got to her. And as the years went by and we became older our arrangements became more fluid and the festive season got even more disjointed because Brian and Dean would go one way while I went the other. I missed being with my brothers on Christmas Day and would often just see them for an hour when we all visited our nan together before heading off on our way to opposing parents.

Children, however, are adaptable and it didn't take me long to realise that Christmas in two homes had another consequence that was not so upsetting – two lots of presents! In fact, having two homes meant two lots of everything: two lots of clothes, two lots of toys and separate parents to play off against each other. Like any other typical child, I soon learned that there were advantages to being from a broken home and I began to practise the art of parental manipulation. If I couldn't get something from one parent, I'd try and get it from the other and I craftily made them compete against each other for my attention.

My methods were not always subtle though, especially when I made accusations – false, of course – of cruelty or neglect or whatever against one parent to the other. It didn't help my cause when, as the years went by, the relationship between Mum and Dad thawed and they started to talk. They started to compare notes.

I arrived back at Mum's one day in floods of tears with an evil plan brewing in my mind. I had rowed over something petty with Dad and I wanted to get him in trouble so I made up a story.

'Dad battered me,' I sniffed. 'We were arguing and he hit me.'

Dad has never laid a finger on me in my life yet there I was sobbing to Mum and accusing him of attacking me.

Mum was livid.

'He did *what*?' she roared. 'Right, that's it. We are going to sort this out right now.'

She called Dad and ordered him round to the house to face the charges. At this point I started to feel a little uneasy. If I didn't think fast the whole plan was going to unravel because it was going to be Dad's word against mine – and we both knew that he hadn't touched me.

We waited anxiously while my dad drove over, Mum getting worked up and me getting increasingly worried.

When he came in the accusations started right away.

'Why did you hit her?' Mum said angrily.

'I didn't,' Dad replied. They both turned to look at me, questioning expressions on their faces.

'Well?' they asked in unison.

'He battered me... with a sock.' It was a desperate effort but the best I could think of under such pressure.

'A sock?' Dad said, almost laughing, but clearly still angry about being summoned to a kangaroo court on a Saturday afternoon. I explained that when Dad was ordering me to tidy my room he had flicked a sock at me in frustration. It was the truth, I had just exaggerated a little.

That little episode earned me a telling off from both Mum and Dad.

It was just as well that they began to get on better because if they hadn't I would have run rings around them.

Although they didn't see each other very frequently, when they did they were cordial and friendly. Whenever Mum needed something done in the house Dad would help out and when she was short of cash and Dad's business was doing well he would give her extra money. But it took quite a few years for them to get to that point.

In my darkest times, when I was adjusting to my life or when I had argued with Mum, which happened more and more as I got older, I would go to the place where I could always find solace and comfort. Where I could speak openly about what I felt and not worry about being judged or about hurting people's feelings – Vinnie's stable.

He was the first one I confided in after my parents split. I remember the conversation. Vinnie was lying down on his warm wood-shavings bed and the way he curled round made him just like a comfy sofa. Mum had taken me to the stables and was outside talking to the owner. I crept into Vinnie's stall and leaned back into the soft crook of his flank.

'Vinnie,' I said quietly, 'Mum and Dad aren't together any more.'

His big horsey breaths rocked me to and fro. He lay still, fixing me with those beautiful, caring eyes and listening to every word I said.

Tears ran down the side of my face but I let them flow unchecked. 'Dad doesn't live with us now and he has to pick me up in a big car and take me to his new place, and I don't like it, it's strange and none of my things are there and I don't see him every day and Dean and Brian are there too, and I'm sad. I wish things were the way they used to be.' I took a deep gulp of air – my words had come out all in a jumble, but it was such a relief to finally be able to let out all the emotion I had been feeling.

Vinnie gave a comforting snort and I breathed in his lovely, warm smell that was mixed in with the wood shavings he lay on. I knew that Vinnie understood, deep down. Having vented my feelings, I suddenly felt exhausted, my eyelids felt heavy and it was there where Mum found me, asleep against Vinnie's side, with that big old beautiful horse watching over me.

As the years went by Mum started dating again and had a few serious boyfriends. I didn't really get on with any of them. I missed my dad and resented anyone trying to take his place. I would argue with them all and whenever they tried to tell me to do something I would use the line: 'You can't tell me what to do, you're not my dad.' Then I'd go back to Dad and tell him that they had been horrible to me. Dad would get annoyed and warn them against raising a voice to me.

One boyfriend in particular used to really get on my nerves and I'm sure the feeling was mutual. I was never a tidy child, my room was always a mess of clothes I had not hung up and toys I had not put away, and this wound him up. Perhaps I should have listened to him as I'd have to learn to live in cramped quarters when I was married! But at the time, he irritated me so badly and I didn't want to do a single thing that he said. Matters came to a head one day when once again I refused to tidy my room. I had been preoccupied and neglected my chores because I had a new thing to care for. An egg! I had found it tucked in a hay bale on Vinnie's farm and made it my mission to save it, hatch it and raise whatever little chick was growing inside it.

I brought it back home and turned out the kitchen cupboards to find a suitable container to keep it in. I chose a cup and lined it with tissue paper and cotton wool to keep it warm. I kept it in my room and each morning and afternoon I carefully turned it, checking it regularly to see if any cracks were appearing. I was obsessed with that egg.

But then the row with Mum's boyfriend happened.

It began as usual with an order to put my things away.

'No,' I argued. 'I don't want to.'

'Just do it, Sam, it looks like a pigsty in here,' he said gesturing around the room.

'Don't tell me what to do, I only take orders from my dad, and you are not my dad,' I yelled back.

Then he noticed the egg. He'd seen what a fuss I had been making of it and knew how important that egg was to me so he picked it up out of its cosy nest and held it to my face between his thumb and forefinger.

'See this,' he hissed. 'If you don't tidy up this bloody room, I'm going to scramble your egg and whatever is inside it.'

I screamed in horror and as I did he dropped the egg. It tumbled through the air in slow motion as I swooped to try and catch it, but I wasn't quick enough. It fell to the floor with a dull, wet splat. Yolk and white seeped into the carpet.

'My egg!' I cried. 'You killed my egg!'

Looking back I don't know which of us was the more childish, me for refusing to tidy my room or him for threatening a child with an egg – perhaps I should have known better than to rile him up, but I was only a little girl while he was as grown man. I had a right to be childish, I was a child, after all. I was so devastated that I cried and sulked for days. Mum was with that man for several years but eventually it ended.

Relationships with Dad's girlfriends fared better. I got on well with Jamie. I remember the first time I met her. She was thin and had tight curly hair. She was sitting on the end of the sofa with a glass of wine and I thought she looked dead posh. We have had our moments over the years. But as a child I must have been a handful. I had begun to develop an attitude towards authority. I didn't like being told what to do by anyone and would often yo-yo backwards and forwards between parents, either because I had been ordered out as a result of some row or another or because I had walked out... as a result of some row or another.

At heart, though, I was and always have been a daddy's girl. I missed Dad when I wasn't with him and I missed my brothers, who had been such a big part of my early life. When Dad settled down with Jamie and they had Tiffany and Morgan, his home always seemed more stable.

And I know he missed me. His fight for custody after the split was not just out of a sense of duty. When we weren't arguing he really valued having me with him. Like Mum, Dad is not prone to emotional outbursts, he's an easy-going man with a calm manner and a great sense of humour. During those dark times while we all adjusted to our new lives I only ever saw him cry twice and both of those were because of the situation he found himself in – partially estranged from his daughter.

On the first occasion I had been staying at his house for the weekend and it was Saturday evening. We'd had our tea together and I had crept upstairs to play in my bedroom. I'm not sure what game I was playing, probably Narnia because I'd climbed into my new wardrobe and was jumping up and down inside it, imagining I was fighting off the White Witch's army of demons and monsters. It must have been a good game because at one point I felt the wood underneath me give way with a sharp snap. I stopped, horrified. My feet had gone straight through the base.

*Dad's going to kill me*, I thought to myself worriedly, and gingerly climbed out of the wardrobe and into bed. I knew I was in trouble and started crying. Dad came upstairs to see what was wrong.

'I want to go home to Mum,' I told him through sniffles. I didn't want to get told off and thought that if I could get out of the house he wouldn't find out that I'd broken the wardrobe. Of course he would have discovered it sooner or later but, when you're a kid, your first impulse if to run from trouble and hope it never catches up with you.

He couldn't understand why I wanted to go.

'But we were supposed to watch telly together and go out tomorrow,' he said sadly.

'I don't want to be here, I want to go home to Mum,' I repeated.

Dad looked utterly crestfallen. He hadn't seen me all week and had planned out our whole weekend. He didn't want to upset me any more than I already was and he was torn between granting my wish and keeping me there for himself.

'We better get your things then,' he said quietly. He turned to the wardrobe to start packing up my weekend bag and saw the damaged floor.

'Is this why you want to go?' he asked with his back to me.

'Yes,' I sniffed.

When he turned back to me there were tears in his eyes.

'Oh, Sam,' he soothed, 'it was only a cheap wardrobe, don't worry about it.'

He sat down on the edge of the bed and wrapped his strong arms around me. When he looked at me his eyes were moist and red.

'Are you upset about the wardrobe, Daddy?' I asked.

'Of course I'm not,' he said. 'I'm upset because I thought you wanted to leave because you didn't want to be with me here.'

About six months later there was a two-week period where I didn't see him. I can't remember why. It was the longest we had been apart since the split and when I saw him he grabbed me and squeezed me so hard I could barely breathe. Once again I saw a tell-tale glistening in his eyes. Every little kid thinks their parents are invincible, but of course they're human and have their vulnerabilities, but it takes a while to discover that for yourself, and you never forget the first time you see your parents cry.

# 3

## Child's Play

When I was five years old I started primary school and was thankful for the opportunity to get away from the problems at home. It had only been a year since Mum and Dad separated and there were still bad feelings between them at that point, so I looked forward to the days in class concentrating on schoolwork and playing with my friends.

I went to Legh Vale Primary School in Haydock and soon got to grips with school life. I proudly put on my baby blue and burgundy uniform each morning and skipped happily to classes. The school was a normal primary of just a few hundred pupils. It felt safe and secure and the teachers there cared about us and our education. While I was there the school won a big national award for being one of the best in the country and we had a special assembly where the head teacher congratulated us all on our hard work.

Lessons were fun and interesting and I was particularly good at maths. I loved doing sums and working out arithmetic problems. The teachers were pleased with my progress and there were rarely complaints when it came time for parents' evening.

Although most of the teachers at school were lovely, my class tutor was an odd man. He would pick a favourite member of the class each week to sit at his desk and they would have to trot around with him for that week like his little pet. It was supposed to be a treat but it felt weird. He wore novelty ties and socks with cartoon characters on them – which isn't really that strange in itself – but he'd also get enthused by the most unusual things and we would sit there dumbstruck and bemused by his behaviour. I remember once he decided to do a photography project and made the whole class lie on the floor in a circle, arranged like petals on a flower so he could take an arty picture of us all.

The school also offered another new aspect to life: girls. Having grown up with Brian and Dean it was a new experience to be around the same sex and although the school was mixed, I found it easier to make friends with girls much more readily than I did with boys. Having constantly been the victim of my brothers' pranks made me wary of boys and it was a relief to be able to hang around with friends who weren't plotting to scare me in some way.

My best friend at school was Danielle. We met up on the first day when we sat next to each other in our new classroom and we soon became inseparable. Danielle, like me, had a slight frame, a smiley face and dark hair. She also had a sense of mischievous fun and a wicked side that showed itself through pranks and practical jokes. We used to sit together and giggle whenever our teacher went off on one of his excitable rants.

We also met up after classes or at the weekends at one another's homes, cajoling our mums into becoming a taxi service between the two houses. Danielle and I spent most weekends together and we'd have regular sleepovers, alternating houses on Saturday nights. We'd stay up late watching films with the sound turned down so our parents didn't hear and scoff crisps and sweets under the covers. We played adventure games, dressed up and made each other laugh through the night.

The other interest we shared was football. Danielle was a member of the school team the same as me and every weekend we would pull on our school football kit and run out on to the pitch for a game. Legh Vale was part of the local girls' league and we did well season after season. We even made it to into the local newspaper when our school struck a deal with a neighbouring school to use their AstroTurf pitches to train on. Both teams, which were usually rivals, were lined up for the photograph and I was first in line at the newsagent's a few days later when the article came out. I wasn't bothered about what the reporter wrote about us, I just wanted to see the photo of Danielle and me and the rest of the team. I felt as if I were famous and took it into school to show everybody, not thinking that of course they had all gone out and bought a copy too.

The school became so well known for its football achievements that one day we had a visit from some Everton players. I can't recall who they were, probably some teenagers from the reserve side made to go out in the community to promote the team. I do remember the reaction from some of the Liverpool supporters in the school, though. There is a bitter rivalry between the two clubs and the boys who supported the Reds made sure the Everton lads knew it.

As well as football at the weekends I still had Vinnie. I went with Mum to feed and muck him out twice a day and that also became part of my Christmas Day routine. In between being shuttled around between homes I would go and see Vinnie and take him some Christmas treats. And by then I was beginning to compete in junior horse shows as well. I was too young for show-jumping but I'd ride around on him in front of the judges and on my bedroom wall I proudly lined up the rosettes and ribbons I had won.

Regularly at the weekend I would pull on my jodhpurs, my riding hat and my smart blue blazer and go with Mum or Dad to a local show. It must have looked odd when we rode out into the riding ring. All the other girls were on pretty little ponies and then me and Vinnie would appear; a tiny girl on a mammoth horse. I didn't care. Sitting high up on my steed I felt on top of the world.

That all changed when I was six, however. Mum and Dad were both at an event I was riding in. Everything was going well and Vinnie was his usual relaxed self when a horse near him got spooked by something and began to rear up. It set off all the other horses as well and suddenly I could feel Vinnie tense up beneath me and become skittish. Within seconds, Vinnie started bucking – it felt like being on a roller coaster.

'Whoa, boy,' I soothed. But it was no good. All the confidence I had built up over the years quickly drained away. I suddenly realised just how small I was compared to the animal beneath me.

I couldn't hold on for long. My little hands having lost the grip on the reins, I slipped to the side and fell off with a thump. I lay on the ground dazed, looking up at Vinnie. Although I was winded, I was otherwise unhurt and got to my feet and grabbed the reins. Vinnie calmed down and I stroked his flank to reassure him everything was okay.

Mum and Dad had both been watching the drama and sprinted over to make sure I was all right.

Mum brushed the dust off my back and went to help me back in the saddle but Dad was having none of it.

'She's not getting back on that,' he said. 'I've said it before: that horse is far too big for her. This proves it, it is dangerous.'

Mum and me both tried to argue but it was no good. Dad was probably right: when I was lying prone on the ground all Vinnie had to do was inadvertently bring a hoof down on me and I would have been in serious trouble. Dad was only trying to protect me, but at the time I hated him for it. There was no room for negotiation: my riding days were over until I was bigger.

I was devastated but would still go and see Vinnie each day and help to look after him. He was still alive all those years later when I married and has always been part of my life.

As primary school progressed home life settled down, and what with friends, football and horses I started to miss my brothers less and less. When we did get together it was still like the old days and we'd start where we had left off, rowing, fighting and arguing. I made it my mission to get them into trouble whenever I could and they responded in kind. It must have driven our parents mad. More often than not we would come to blows.

One day Dean and I were at Mum's and were arguing as normal, probably about something irrelevant and petty. On that particular day, Dean must have wound me up more than usual because I decided to punch him. I clenched my fists and with all my strength I belted him in his stomach. I could see his cheeks puff out and eyes widen and I knew I had hurt him. A warm glow of satisfaction spread through me. Dean was bent double in front of me, clutching his tummy. But it was a short-lived victory. It took him a few seconds to recover and when he straightened up I saw the look in his eye that I had learnt meant it was time to run. He roared and lunged at me and I scarpered. A few seconds later he caught me and started pummelling me just as Mum stormed into the room.

'Dean! Stop hitting Sam,' she demanded.

Dean looked at her, wounded, his hand raised in a fist over my head. 'But she hit me first.'

'I never, you're lying,' I lied.

Mum chose to believe me and ordered Dean outside

to cool off. He skulked off through the door and muttered: 'That's it, I'm leaving,' as he went.

Behind Mum's back, I stuck my tongue out at him as he left the room.

Over the next hour I basked in the glow of a rare victory while Mum continued with her housework. We assumed that Dean was sulking outside. But as the afternoon wore on we realised that the house was strangely quiet.

'Where is Dean?' said Mum. 'He's been playing outside for ages.'

We checked around the house and in the front and back gardens but there was no sign of him. We went back inside and looked in every room. Then we checked the gardens again and Mum walked up and down the road looking for him. All the while she was becoming increasingly worried. Brian was home too and helped to look with us. We did another check of the house and turned each room upside down, looking in cupboards and wardrobes.

'If this is a game, Dean, it is time to stop now and come out,' Mum called.

After a few hours she had become frantic with worry. We got in the car and drove round and round the neighbourhood. She called friends and family, she checked with

Dad and he came looking too. The horror of the situation dawned on us all. Dean had disappeared. He could have run off and got stuck in a drain somewhere or snatched off the street. He could be in mortal danger – he could even be dead.

As late afternoon came round Mum called the police. Within half an hour they turned up at the house and questioned us about when and where we last saw Dean and some of the places he might have gone. We had checked them all. Mum gave the officers a photograph of him so they could copy it and circulate it around. Dean was officially a missing person and the police assured us that in the huge majority of cases, children who run off turn up safe and well after a few hours. But it had been several hours since Dean walked out. The sun was going down and it was getting dark outside. The temperature was dropping and Dean had only been wearing a light sweatshirt when he stomped out. Mum was afraid that he was going to freeze to death.

All that night the house was a buzz of activity as it became the centre of the search operation to find my brother. I felt awful. If I hadn't hit him in the first place and then got him into trouble with my lies he would still be with us. I knew that if he had been abducted or had suffered a terrible accident somewhere, it was all my fault.

I slept fitfully, dreaming of Dean alone, cold, scared and lost in a remote wood somewhere, whimpering for his family, his home and his warm bed. What had I done?

The next morning, as I woke up, I at first assumed I was still dreaming because I could hear Dean's voice coming from somewhere. As I wiped the sleep from my eyes I realised that it was no dream: Dean was back. His voice was coming from the kitchen downstairs. My heart leapt for joy as I kicked off the covers and ran downstairs to see him. He was sitting at the table having cornflakes. Mum was fussing around him but there was a funny look on her face. I would have imagined that she would be happy to see him; instead she looked slightly annoyed.

'Dean, where have you been?' I asked. I wanted to hear all about his adventure. 'What happened to you, did the police find you?'

Dean shrugged. 'I haven't been anywhere, no one found me and nothing happened,' he replied sheepishly.

I was confused. Then Mum explained. Dean was right, he hadn't gone off anywhere; he had played a trick on us that has become a family legend. After he stomped out of my room he did go outside but then he decided to teach us all a lesson and crept back in, and stealthily went up to his bedroom. He quietly collected up an old duvet and some blankets and rolled himself into them like a cigar. Then he rolled himself under his bed and wedged himself right at the back near the wall where he couldn't be seen. And then he waited... and waited.

Whoever checked his room would have just seen an old blanket stuffed under the bed. When we went out looking for him he must have shuffled back out to use the loo and then got back into his cosy hideaway and fallen asleep there. He came down in the morning like nothing had happened. He'd been hiding out under our noses for almost 24 hours. He was proud of himself and, by the time he resurfaced, Mum had had such an awful night, continually checking on the progress of the police search, that she was too exhausted and emotionally drained to be mad at him for long. She was just glad he was safe.

A few years later Dean did another disappearing act on a holiday in Holland. We had gone there with my dad and his then girlfriend. It was a lovely holiday; we stayed in a holiday park in a chalet and spent days out on bikes enjoying the local area. The advantage of having older brothers was that I was allowed more freedom than other girls my age because I would tag along with them and they knew they had to keep an eye on me. Dean and I had found a field with a huge tree in the middle of it, and it became our special place. We'd cycle there, sit in the shade and talk about the kind of stuff kids talk about. Then one day Dean had an argument and did what he often did – he stormed off. After a while Dad was starting to get anxious and went off looking for him. I knew instinctively where he would be and grabbed my bike. Maybe I remembered the drama of the last time he disappeared and wanted to make amends for my part in it. Whatever the reason, I was determined to go and bring him back.

I pedalled across the holiday park to our special field and sure enough there he was, stretched out under the tree. I told him Dad was getting worried and that it would be better off if he came back. It didn't happen very often but in that situation Dean listened and he came back with me.

Summer holidays were always fun. We usually went on holiday with Dad but Mum took us on trips too and some years it worked out that we had two holidays abroad. Dad could often be impulsive when it came to organising trips away. If he had a good few months with his business he would organise a holiday on the spur of the moment.

'Pack your bags, Sam. We're going to Cyprus tomorrow,' he would say on the phone. We stayed in hotels and mobile homes on big continental campsites and would spend days splashing around at the beach or in the pool.

In Ibiza he took us for a cruise in an amazing glass-bottomed boat and I sat there open-mouthed and spellbound looking at the colourful fish that flitted past beneath us, their iridescent scales glittering in the sunlight that filtered down from the surface. They looked like beautiful butterflies. When I got back to our chalet that night I sat down with my felt-tip pens and tried to draw them all from memory. They were so beautiful I didn't ever want to forget what they looked like.

As the years went on and I grew older I started to become aware of how much I was changing. Even before I left primary school I had started to look different in a swimsuit. I became more conscious of the way I looked; on holiday I would take more care of my hair and my appearance and when I packed I would choose carefully what to take. The trackies and baggy T-shirts were gradually replaced with trendy clothes. The little tomboy who used to climb trees and would rather turn up at mufti day dressed as a police officer than a fairy was fading into the past, replaced by a girl who liked to wear dresses and experimented with make-up. I was becoming more aware of how I looked and, each month, when I looked in the mirror, I realised that even though I was still just a little girl at heart, my body was changing.

I was starting to grow up.

# 4

# Everything Changes

The shop was heaving with people rifling through racks of clothes, looking for that perfect outfit for a Saturday night. Dance music pumped through the sound system so loud you could feel the bass vibrate through your chest. I stood there looking around and blinking in wonder.

TopShop was a totally alien environment to me. Most of my clothes came from JD Sports, but this was a proper fashion store and it was a whole new world. As we stepped inside the store, Mum had a grin on her face. She loved to shop, but mostly she was pleased because finally I had started to show an interest in what I wore. She had a shopping buddy at last.

After years of being cajoled to be more feminine, at nine years of age my inner girlie finally won the battle with the tomboy part of my personality. Since living apart from my brothers and my dad, I no longer had a day-to-day male influence in my life. And I had also grown and changed. I wanted to look more like a young lady. Mum loved taking me round the shops and although I wasn't quite ready for a full-on makeover, I started to wear dresses and more girlie tops.

'Try this on, Sam, it'll look amazing,' she encouraged, holding up a short denim skirt and strappy top.

'That looks cool,' I smiled, grabbing it from her and trotting off to the changing room like a proper teenager.

I'd started to enjoy going shopping and took a keen interest in fashion. If there was a magazine lying around the house I'd pick it up and have a flick through to see what pop stars such as Kylie and Christina Aguilera were wearing. I started to listen to their music too and the horsey posters on my bedroom wall gradually got replaced by posters of celebrities such as Nelly and Pink. I still visited Vinnie but my interests were expanding.

I felt very grown up trying on clothes in shops for older kids and teenagers. Now, during sleepovers with Danielle, the midnight feasts and ghost stories we used to scare ourselves with were replaced by hair and make-up sessions. I'd rifle through Mum's drawers to 'borrow' some lippy for when Danielle came over and would clumsily apply it, then wipe it off quickly when I heard Mum's footsteps outside.

And my fashion sense wasn't the only thing that was developing as I neared the final year of primary school. My body had also started to grow. I was no longer a scrawny flat-chested little kid. I was an early developer and had started to develop a teenager's body, well ahead of the rest of the girls in the school. Mum bought me my first bra and I was a B cup. Although I was more aware of styles and fashions, the changes in my body were making me increasingly confused. I wanted to look nice, but I didn't want to draw attention to myself. While I knew that what was happening to my body was completely natural and normal, I felt uncomfortable because I was the first girl in the school to go through those changes and that made me self-conscious.

I had always loved PE and football. I had played football for the school for years but I was beginning to dread any form of group physical activity. I started to find excuses not to go to football practice and to skip games lessons. I pretended to have headaches or a twisted ankle, anything to save the embarrassment of undressing in front of people.

When I couldn't come up with a plan to get out of PE, the teachers would have to rush me to get ready because I would always be the last out of the changing room. I messed around and chatted to friends while they got ready just so I could be the last one to get my kit on in an empty room where no one could see me take off my vest. I didn't want to wear anything that showed off the bras I was wearing because no one else was wearing them, and I felt that somehow they made me different from the other kids. All the other girls looked tiny compared to me and I wished I could stop growing. I wanted my old flat chest back.

The other girls would make comments; a lot of them were intrigued and even envious. We were all the same age and we were all changing, it was no big secret. It just seemed that the changes were happening faster and on a bigger scale to my body than they were to anyone else in the school. I grew out of tops every few weeks and I'd struggle into tight vests underneath my uniform to try to flatten down my figure.

But no matter how hard I tried, I couldn't hide what was happening to me and what made it worse was that the boys at school were beginning to notice. I would catch them staring and they'd raise their eyes to mine and shuffle off, embarrassed that I had caught them looking. I'd hear someone whisper something to his friend in the hallway as I walked past and try not to look back as they started to snigger. I'd never experienced bullying before and all this extra, unwanted attention made me feel like a freak. I didn't want to be who I was.

For years the school had been a haven for me. I had made loads of friends and enjoyed each day. But now it seemed to me that school was a hostile place and suddenly I felt I was different, an outsider.

As I neared the end of primary school it became worse as I continued to grow. In my last year at Legh Vale I was constantly singled out by boys who would no longer try and hide their sense of amusement. They'd point openly at me if I was in PE lessons and they called me names.

'You should be on Page Three,' they'd laugh if I was playing netball.

The jibes stung and although I tried to give as good as I got, I went home at the end of each day feeling utterly miserable.

'What's the matter?' Mum would ask as I walked in with red eyes because I'd been crying on the way home. I wouldn't answer, I'd just run upstairs to my room, and bury my head in my pillow and weep. I was embarrassed by my body and I didn't want to draw any more attention to it than there was already. I didn't think anyone would understand so I kept my mouth shut. I loved school in the first years but the constant bullying and taunts about my body made me deeply unhappy.

I kept what I was feeling from my parents and must have hidden it well because they did not question me, and my dress sense began to change back into the tracksuits and baggy tops that I had worn when I was a tomboy as I tried to cover myself up.

I confided in Danielle.

'I hate the way I look,' I sniffed. 'Everybody stares, the boys call me names and I get bullied. I don't know what to do.'

Danielle looked at me with worry in her eyes. 'It'll be okay,' she said. 'You won't be the odd one out much longer – we're all going to go through it soon.'

Her words comforted me a bit, but in fact the situation got worse as time went on: after a while it was not just boys my own age – nine- and ten-year-olds – who noticed me and my new body: older men started looking at me as well. And that turned my stomach. One day I was walking through the supermarket with Mum and as I walked past one of the shelf-stackers I caught his eyes darting down to look at my chest. They lingered there far too long and as I passed him he looked me in the eye. He had a horrible unsettling look on his face, a sick look of longing.

*I'm just a kid*, I thought. *You're disgusting*. Once I had seen that type of look, I began to notice it more and more and it horrified and frightened me. Those men seemed to be like parasites, feeding their fantasies by staring at my body. Their glances made me feel dirty and ashamed.

One day, on the way to school, matters came to a head. It was mufti day and we could wear whatever we wanted. I got the bus to school that day and decided that I wanted to wear something pretty, rather than a baggy T-shirt. I couldn't hide away from the world for ever and the injustice of having to feel like an outsider was getting to me so much that I decided to make a stand and try to be proud of who I was and what I looked like.

So I reached into my wardrobe in the morning and picked out a trendy tight-fitting top and a pair of jeans. I looked in the mirror after I changed and liked what I saw. It wasn't my fault that I looked like a teenager, why should I be ashamed?

Mum even told me that I looked nice when I went down for breakfast so by the time I got to the bus stop I was in a better mood than I had been for weeks.

I waited a few minutes and the bus pulled up. I climbed on and walked over to the driver, dropping 20p in his cash tray.

'Half please,' I said.

'What?' he laughed.

I stared at him blinking. He was wearing a grubby uniform and his squinty eyes peered at me. His hair was greasy and plastered to his forehead underneath his driver's cap.

'Can I have a half fare, please?' I repeated.

He laughed in a sneering, grunting way. And then slowly and purposefully he lowered his eyes and he looked at my chest. I squirmed. It felt as if I was being undressed in public. My cheeks flushed with embarrassment and then, while he was still staring at my top, he said, 'Well, *they're* not a half, are they? They're bigger than my wife's.'

I was horrified, but by now there were people behind me waiting to get on the bus. A man in the queue laughed and an elderly woman tutted.

I felt totally exposed. Everyone was looking at me. It was the final straw.

'You pervert!' I screamed. 'You are sick, I am going to report you for what you just said!'

I burst into tears, turned, pushed my way off the bus and past the queue and ran back home.

Mum was annoyed that I hadn't gone to school, but after she had calmed down I told her what had happened and later that day I told Dad. He was furious and stormed off to find the driver who had insulted me. Apparently Dad tracked him down and had a go at him. I never found out what happened to the man. It was a disgraceful thing to say to a young child.

And so that was how my last year of primary school went. I was miserable and dodged the bullies every day. I went from being an athletic, involved member of the school community to a shy, withdrawn loner who was starting to develop a chip on her shoulder and an attitude to match.

I was getting moody and sometimes aggressive. In my last year at school I even got in a fight with one of the boys. He had been calling me names so I decided to fight back with my fists and I punched him in the face. It was a stain on my record but by that point I had realised that sometimes if you want to beat the bullies you need to fight fire with fire.

Towards the last months of my final year I learnt that I had got a place in the local high school, Haydock High. It was the main school in the area and the one most of my classmates were going to as well. Danielle would be starting with me, so I knew I would have an ally there. We kept our fingers crossed that we would be in the same form and as summer term ended I started to look forward to the long holidays.

As I became older I was allowed increasingly more freedom, especially by Mum. Most of the kids my age had to be back in for early curfews and when I was at Dad's I still had to be home early, he was quite strict, but Mum let me stay out a bit later and I was meeting more kids around town to hang out with. Some of them were several years older than me but it didn't seem to matter away from school. And my older brothers would always keep a watchful eye on me, too.

I had mixed feelings on the last day of term at Legh Vale. I'd had some wonderful times there and made some lifelong friends. Danielle and I are still in contact today. It had also given me a focus after my parents split up. But my last year there had been soured by bullying and name-calling and when I walked out of the gates for the final time part of me was glad to be embarking on a new chapter of life. And besides, it was the summer holidays, which meant long days with my friends and the freedom to roam around the town and surrounding neighbourhoods.

I was excited about the weeks ahead. But I wasn't aware of just how life-changing that summer would turn out to be.

# 5

# Attack

The summer between primary school and high school should have been one of the most memorable of my life, for good reasons. For most children it is a milestone, a time when they grow noticeably and say goodbye to their younger years. It's a time when some of the naivety and innocence of childhood is shed.

But when I try and think about that time my mind goes blank, as if I have erased as much of it from my memory as I can. I suppose it is a kind of defence mechanism. My brain has blanked out the whole summer to try and protect me from what happened during it.

Even the memories of that one horrific event are sketchy and I'm glad of that because I don't want to remember it in any detail. All I can do is explain what I am able to recall.

After primary school and before the adventure of secondary school had begun, I spent much of the holidays hanging out in Haydock, nearby Earlestown and Blackbrook, where my Dad lived. There were parks and fields dotted around the area because, although the towns were busy enough, they are still surrounded by countryside and quite often I'd walk through fields and parks to get to my destination. I never gave safety a second thought. I had grown up in the area and it was safe. There was a sense of community and people knew their neighbours and watched out for each other.

On the day it happened I had been hanging out in Haydock with friends. As it was getting late, I said goodbye and started to walk home.

There was some open parkland nearby that I often used as a shortcut and as dusk fell I decided to walk through it and save myself some time.

The route led me through some secluded paths sheltered from the open land by trees and bushes and because it was around 9 p.m., certain areas I had to walk through were darkened by shadow where the setting sun could not penetrate. I had made the same journey many times before and had never worried. But this time was different. Instinct told me that I wasn't alone. I hadn't seen anyone nearby as I walked through the open parkland but I felt a presence: someone was there with me. I started to feel frightened and quickened my pace.

The first thing I heard was the crack of branches as a man pushed through the bushes in front of me. It happened so quickly I had no time to react. I jumped and gasped and the flood of adrenalin in my system was so extreme my legs buckled with the shock of it. I had no time to turn and within a split second he had grabbed me and slapped me hard across the face. He was bearing down on me and the fright sparked my asthma, which had been under control for years. Suddenly I felt my chest constrict and I was struggling for breath. He put his hand over my mouth. He smelt of sweat, booze and cigarettes and the stench and the fear made me retch.

'Keep your mouth shut and you won't get hurt,' he lied.

He was about 20 years old and spoke with a Manchester accent. I noticed the dark mark of a tattoo on his arm but I couldn't make out the design in the gloom. He wore a grey hooded top and grey tracksuit bottoms. His eyes were slits of pure evil. They were boring into me. He grabbed my chest with his free hand and roughly manhandled me. I tried to struggle but the messages from my brain couldn't reach my limbs. Every sinew in me was screaming 'run, run', but I was frozen to the spot.

I couldn't even speak, I couldn't plead or scream. I was petrified. My heart felt like it was going to burst out of my chest and all I could hear was the blood coursing through my veins and the sounds of his animal grunts as he roughly bundled me to the ground, kicking at the backs of my knees to make them buckle. I tried to resist, to stay on my feet, but he was too strong.

'I'll cut your throat, you bitch,' he hissed. 'They won't find you for days.'

Whimpers escaped from behind his hand as I felt him claw at me. I couldn't feel anything: I went numb. I tried to make myself pass out so I wouldn't have to feel what he was doing.

He forced himself on me and in a few short horrific minutes he violated me. After, he kicked me so hard in the stomach I was sick. I lay on the ground shaking, my hair matted with vomit.

'I know who you are and where you live,' he sneered. 'If you tell anyone about this I'll hunt you down.'

'Please,' I begged, 'just leave me alone.'

As he left I heard him laugh.

Cuts on my arms and back from the rough ground oozed blood. I couldn't even cry – I was in deep shock.

I don't know how long I was there. Time dissolved. At some point, I got up and staggered home in the darkness.

My mind was racing with questions. Why had I taken that route home? Why hadn't I fought back? Why hadn't

I lashed out or bitten him? It was my fault. I was stupid. I had invited trouble and it had found me. And I was terrified, too. How did the attacker know who I was? Had he been watching me? What if he was watching me now to see what I did?

By the time I got home I knew I wasn't going to tell anyone. I felt ashamed and ran upstairs and got into a bath where I scrubbed myself over and over again until my skin was red raw. All that mattered was removing every speck of him from me. Once I had done that I could try and forget and move on.

I took deep breaths and tried to calm the storm that was roaring through my mind. What had just happened? Surely I should be going to the police station and making a statement? But my resolve not to tell anyone held firm. I felt that somehow I was to blame for what had happened to me.

That night I climbed into bed and lay in the dark shaking uncontrollably. Whenever I closed my eyes I saw his face hidden by shadows and felt his clammy hand close around my mouth. I fell into a fitful sleep and dreamed that I was running so fast and so freely my feet did not touch the ground. The countryside spun past me in a blur and I felt light and free.

When I woke the next morning my heart felt dark. There were bruises all over my body and my limbs felt like they were made of concrete. It took a huge mental effort just to lift myself out of bed.

Something had been snatched away from me, something I would never get back. I made a vow to myself that I would never let anyone else hurt me. What happened that day would remain my cross to bear alone. I would learn from the lesson. I would be more careful in future and I would try to get over it as best I could. I would not let myself be beaten by that disgusting man. And the best way to defeat him was to treat the night before as if it never happened, to erase it totally from my life and to move on. I couldn't stand the thought of police investigations, probing questions, court cases and identity parades. If I went to the police, I felt that it would validate what the man had done to me. If I ignored it all and blanked it from my life I would not have to even acknowledge it.

I know now that I was in shock but at the time it seemed like I was thinking logically. I blamed myself: I felt that I was silly and I got what I deserved. Even today I blame myself. I didn't want people to feel sorry for me, I didn't want their sympathy or pity. What happened was awful and wrong and if I could go back in time of course I would have done things differently. I would have made sure I was safe in my bedroom at home watching television, rather than walking home on my own at dusk through a field. But I reasoned that there were people who have had much, much worse things happen to them.

I couldn't change it, I didn't have a time machine or a magic wand so I just wanted to forget and move on and in the following days that is how I learned to cope. I put the events of that evening in a little box and locked it securely at the back of my mind. I thought that would work. But sometimes the lock on that box popped open and the nightmares began.

I stayed away from home for the rest of the holidays as much as I could. I went back for meals and to sleep but I didn't want to be around my mum or my dad, just in case they noticed something was different in me and started questioning me. The whole world felt different. I couldn't see how anything could ever be the same again.

When school finally started I was glad to go: it meant a change of environment, a chance to get away and perhaps make a fresh start and leave the old me behind – the one that over the summer months had become a victim.

The first day at Haydock High I arranged to meet Danielle at the school gates. We were both nervous and had on our brand-new blue checked uniforms. The school seemed enormous. There were around 1,500 pupils and we were lost in the sea of children. The school had its own one-way system to get around and it was a challenge to get from one side of the grounds to the other. We checked the notice board to see if we were going to be in the same form. After what had happened I was hoping with all my might that Danielle would be with me. I needed a friend more than ever.

But as we both looked down the alphabetical list we realised we had been split up. There were other names in my class that I recognised from Legh Vale but none of them were close friends.

Me and Danielle hugged and arranged to meet at break time in the playground and then we turned in opposite directions and walked to our new classes. I looked over my shoulder as Danielle disappeared in a crowd of excited children. I was surrounded by the hustle and bustle of a big school but I felt like a little girl again. I felt totally alone.

# 6

# Gypsy Boy

They say people don't change but the girl who started high school couldn't have been more different from the girl who left primary school, both mentally and physically. A part of me had died in that secluded wood – the part that believed in happy endings and having fun no matter what. At just 11 years of age I felt that I was damaged goods. I was defensive, defiant and guarded, and inside I was a mess of contradictions, confusion and conflicting emotions.

I looked different too. The long hair had gone. My one concession to my mum's hopes for a girlie girl had been cut off. She was horrified. I did it out of defiance. Mum had always forbidden me to have my hair cut but at the time the bob style was in and I wanted to look like the cool girls.

My cousin Lisa was a hairdresser and so one day I went to her salon in town and sat in the chair.

'Can you do a bob with the back shorter than the sides, please?' I asked.

She laughed. 'You're not allowed to have your hair short,' she said.

'No, Mum says it's okay. Honest,' I lied.

Lisa believed me and set to work snipping away at the lustrous locks I had been growing since I could remember. With each snip of the scissors I felt part of the old me slip away and fall to the floor where it lay in a pile of long, silky brunette hair. After 30 minutes of cutting and styling I could barely recognise the girl staring back at me through the mirror.

*Cool*, I thought to myself. It was as if the part of me that was a victim had been cut away like a cancer and it felt good.

'Mum will be dead pleased with that,' I said to Lisa admiring the new style. 'Can you take a picture of the back?'

Lisa took my phone and snapped a photo of the close-cropped nape of my neck. Once I'd paid and left the shop I sent the picture to Mum's phone with the message, 'Guess who?'

I knew it would wind her up and I knew I would be in trouble when I got home but by that stage I had stopped caring. After everything I had been through, getting told off by my parents seemed like an irrelevance, at worst a minor inconvenience.

Mum wasn't happy with me and we argued. It was becoming the normal pattern in our relationship. But what made her more upset than anything was the fact that I hadn't kept a lock of the hair for her as a keepsake.

At school my attitude had changed too. I was seeing less and less of Danielle because we were in separate classes and had a different timetable to each other. I had begun to make a new set of friends, both boys and girls, and my behaviour in class was starting to cause the teachers concern. I would talk through lessons and wasn't interested in learning anything. I rarely did homework and the standard of the work I did do was deteriorating. I disrupted classes and on several occasions the teachers pulled me out of class to try to discipline me. At first they were encouraging. 'Come on, Sam,' they'd urge, 'you're a bright girl, don't waste your talents.'

But it was a big school and the teachers didn't have the time to concentrate on individual troublemakers like me. I soon started to fall by the wayside but I didn't care.

I was particularly friendly with one of the boys in class and we would joke and mess around together. It was totally innocent – after what had happened, boys and relationships were the last things on my mind. That wasn't the case for the rest of the kids in the year, though; all of us were going through that same stage of pre-teenage life where hormones were starting to kick in. My friend began seeing a girl in another class called Amy, and she didn't like the fact I was friends with her new lad.

When we passed each other in the playground or hall-way she shot me dirty looks and I could hear her cuss me under her breath. I started to develop a real dislike for her and when she confronted me one day there was no way I was going to back down.

'My boyfriend fancies you, Norton,' she said. 'You better stay away from him and stop flirting with him.'

I looked her up and down.

'Can you blame him?' I sniffed. 'Look at the state of you.' Secretly I was pleased with myself, it was a good put-down.

She stormed off but later that afternoon the rumours started filtering through the school grapevine: Sam and Amy are having a fight. It was the first I'd heard of it but I wasn't going to be pushed around by anyone. If that's what she wanted then fine, bring it on.

I had learned a valuable lesson in my final year at primary school. If you give the bullies any leeway, they will take advantage of you. And if you let yourself become a victim, you will be victimised again and again. I had already let myself be a victim too many times in my short life and it wasn't going to happen again. This time I was going to fight back.

Dad used to tell Brian and Dean that if someone picks on you and beats you up, you should go back and keep going back until you beat them. With that thought in my mind I walked to the playground where Amy was supposed to be waiting for me with the intention of showing her who was boss.

By now the other pupils had worked themselves into a frenzy. *Fight! Fight!* they chanted as I approached. The crowd parted to let me through and there, in the middle of the baying mob, was Amy. She was waiting for me with an ugly snarl on her face.

I'm not sure if she was expecting some pre-fight banter but she opened her mouth to say something and I punched her in the face. The connection was dead on target and I felt her lip and teeth crunch into my fist. She staggered back and I didn't wait for her to regain her balance. I piled forward, swinging my fists at her face. Some of the shots made contact, some didn't, but after a few seconds under my barrage Amy started to swing back.

We slugged it out for what seemed like ages. We punched and grabbed and kicked while the crowd egged us on. I was fighting on instinct, I wasn't aware of my surroundings or even what I was I doing. I just knew I had to hit this person in front of me and keep hitting her until she stopped hitting me. I was caught up in a red mist of fury and hatred. When an arm reached round my stomach and tried to yank me away from my opponent, I lashed out at that too, trying to scratch it away. I assumed it was one of Amy's friends trying to stop the fight and threw a punch in their direction. Only after my fist connected with the person's face did I realise it wasn't another pupil, but one of the teachers – an elderly lady.

The crowd went quiet, the teacher gasped. I realised I was in deep trouble. Amy had also been restrained and was lashing out at the teacher holding her. There were several adults around us by then and they were all shouting at us and grabbing our arms. I stood there breathing heavily with adrenalin coursing through my veins, staring menacingly at Amy. Blood was trickling from her mouth and nose. I knew that through the fight I'd sent a message to anyone who wanted to try and bully me in the future: don't mess with me.

I felt exhilarated and, as we were both led off to the head teacher's office, I smiled to myself. It felt good to be in control.

I was called in first and the head, a reasonable man

who cared passionately about the school, was willing to hear my side of the story.

'She started it,' I argued. 'She's been picking on me and threatening me, I was just defending myself.'

That wasn't the way he saw it.

'If you don't start behaving yourself, Sam, you'll get in real trouble,' he said. 'We don't want to lose you from this school and I won't let you ruin your chances here.'

Our punishment was to be excluded from classes the next day. We would have to go to a place I called The Room of Shame, where we would be taught separately from the rest of the school. And we would have to do it together.

The next day I was ready to fight all over again. I vowed that at the first snide comment or evil look I would start punching, but as we settled into our seats and the teacher began to reprimand us for what we had done the day before Amy began giggling, and so did I. We both had a common enemy – the teacher who was scolding us. As the day went on we talked to each other and we found we had things in common. We started to joke and lark around and in break time, when we weren't allowed out, we played computer games. Amy became a friend. I'm not sure if the punishment was meant to have that effect but in a roundabout way it worked because we never fought again.

Although my circle of friends was growing, I was never part of the cool set at school. I had begun to develop a reputation as a bit of a rebel and someone to be careful of and, if truth be told, I relished that reputation. I liked to feel powerful. But I had more in common with the normal kids in school, not the ones everyone wanted to be like. My friends were mainly the sort of kids who would have been bullied themselves and I liked to protect them. If anyone said anything to one of my pals, I'd let my fists do the talking. I got in plenty of fights throughout school and I got in plenty of trouble.

At home, Mum and Dad despaired. Brian was at the same school and hated having a notorious sister there. He had changed from the mischievous boy who used to play pranks on me into a quiet, studious pupil. He got his head down and worked hard. He had been in school for two years when I turned up and within a few months people would approach him in the playground and ask: 'Are you Sam Norton's brother?'

It should have been the other way round. Brian was tarred by my reputation and all he wanted was a quiet life. Instead he constantly had to answer for me and my one-girl rebellion.

Another friend at school was Mel. We met up in the first weeks and got friendly quickly. She was bubbly and kind and as I got to know her I realised she was someone I could confide in. I found I could open up to her and talk about how I felt more than anyone else I knew.

I had known her since primary school but back then we never got on well. At Haydock High though we had started talking one day and I discovered what a lovely girl she was. We started hanging around together after school and would stop at each other's houses at weekends when our parents let us.

She was one of the only friends I told about the attack and she was extremely supportive and mature beyond her years.

'You really should go to the doctors or the police,' she advised gently.

'But Mel,' I sighed, 'I don't want to get the authorities involved. I just want to move on with my life. It's been months since it happened and no one will believe me. All I want is to put the whole episode behind me.' She did not push me, she did not judge but said she was there to help me and listen if I needed her and if I ever needed to speak to someone.

I had other friends outside school, many of them were older, and on weekends and some evenings we would hang around in groups and wander around the town. Sometimes we'd go shopping, other times we'd go round each other's houses when our parents were out. We were just normal kids. We didn't cause trouble, even though most of the time we were bored because in Earlestown and Haydock there weren't many things for young teenagers to do. Most of the kids just hung around on the streets or in the youth clubs until they were around 16 and then started venturing into the pubs around town when they looked old enough to get served.

Most weekends there would be different groups of teenagers from different schools and parts of the area milling around. And one group was the traveller boys. You never saw traveller girls but the boys were a common sight.

In and around St Helens and the nearby towns there were several gypsy camps. I didn't know much about them and although there were some traveller lads at school, I didn't have any gypsy friends. But that wasn't because they kept themselves to themselves. Although their community existed alongside but separate from ours, they did integrate in school. I knew a few of them to say hello to. Our area was not like some parts of the country where gypsies are viewed with suspicion and hatred and are shunned by society. They were just part of the working-class area I lived in. There would be groups of them in the local youth club and they'd get along with the non-traveller kids without any trouble.

Of course there were prejudices. There always are when it comes to people who do not live in mainstream society. There were kids at school who would warn you about the gypsies and tell you they were dirty and were con artists and crooks and could never be trusted. I preferred not to judge and to take people as they came. There were just as many so-called normal people who you couldn't trust and who were dirty and bad. I knew that from bitter experience.

So when me and a group of friends were sitting on a bench early one evening and a group of traveller lads came over to say hello, I didn't bat an eyelid. I didn't know them so I didn't say much but my friend Codie knew one of the group – a boy the same age as us named John Thomas. He lived in Earlestown on a site between a skip unloading plant and the railway. He was tall, gangly, self-assured and my first impression was that he fancied himself.

He walked over in a tight vest and leather jacket and started to chat to Codie. I was dressed down for the night in a blue tracksuit with yellow stripes and sat quietly listening to them. By now my hair had started to grow back and was pulled in a ponytail. John Thomas was with another boy and the first thing I noticed about him was his jacket. It was huge! I almost laughed when I saw it. It was bright and padded and swamped the body inside it. Even though whoever was wearing it was taller than me, he looked small and vulnerable inside that coat.

'Did you get that off your dad?' I joked.

'I did, actually,' he answered.

We both laughed nervously.

I looked into his face. He had a wispy growth of facial hair, a strong jaw but soft, sensitive features, but it was his eyes that drew my attention. They were hazel and twinkled in the streetlight with a mischievous sparkle.

'I'm Patrick,' he said. 'But everyone calls me Pat.'

'I'm Samantha – Sam,' I stammered.

And then there was an awkward silence. I felt something strange in my tummy, a churning feeling. He was just as shy as I was but we both realised there was a spark of attraction there. Even though he was a few years older than I was – 14 years of age to my 11 – we were both too young to know what to do about it.

After a short chat, John Thomas said goodbye and the traveller lads walked off. Pat turned and smiled as he walked away.

Codie had seen the meaningful glances that passed between Pat and me and although I didn't realise what it meant, she did.

'He fancies you,' she laughed.

'Don't be stupid,' I said defensively.

I may have been a rebel and one of the naughty kids at school but when it came to boys I was an amateur. I'd never had a boyfriend, I'd never kissed a boy and at that point I didn't want to. But there was something about Pat that played on my mind. I don't know what I expected from a traveller but whatever it was it certainly wasn't Pat. He seemed... well, normal – sweet and polite.

And over the following days I couldn't get him out of my mind. I would catch myself thinking about him and smiling. My friends noticed that I was preoccupied and not my usual bolshie self. Another pal, Holly, guessed what was on my mind.

'You fancy that traveller boy, don't you?' she teased.

'He's nice,' I said coyly.

Holly then hatched a plan. She knew one of Pat's friends, another traveller called Ryan. The next time she saw him she told him to tell Pat that I fancied him and that I would be with a group of others at her house that night if he wanted to come round.

I was invited along to Holly's and later in the evening we were sitting in her front room. Her parents were out and we were messing around and gossiping when the doorbell rang.

Holly sprang up and went to answer it. I heard some voices. Older boys, their voices deeper than the squeaky boys in my year. The lounge door opened and in walked Ryan and Pat.

Our eyes met and we smiled shyly at each other.

I didn't realise at the time but Holly was playing matchmaker and had sprung a trap to get us both together.

With the security of a crowd of people around us we started talking easily and got on well. Pat told me that he didn't go to school. I learned later that he went to an educational centre called Launchpad a few days a week. Instead of full-time education he worked and helped in the family businesses as a landscaper and scrap-metal dealer. I thought that was cool, as I hated school and couldn't wait to leave. But at the time leaving school seemed many years away.

'Let's play a game of spin the bottle,' laughed Holly.

The rules were the same as they have been for generations. If the bottle lands on you, you have the choice of truth or dare. Inevitably the bottle landed on me – Holly was spinning it and I'm certain she made sure it pointed in my direction.

I chose a dare. I wasn't in the mood for a forced confession and, given what had happened to me in the past, I was worried any personal questions might rake up old feelings. I had to make sure my secrets were well and truly buried.

'Kiss Pat,' Holly ordered.

I could feel the blood rising in my cheeks and I flushed red. But I wasn't going to duck out. I looked at Pat and he smiled sheepishly.

'Okay,' he shrugged.

'But not in here in front of you lot,' I said quickly. 'In the hallway.'

Everyone was laughing now and I stood up defiantly and walked into the hallway. Pat followed. We shut the door behind us and stood nervously facing each other. Then he laughed too. His face lit up and he looked at me with those wonderful eyes.

'Well,' he said. 'What are we going to do now?'

I shrugged and we started talking. Conversation with Pat was easy. I told him about school, about the trouble I was getting into and he understood. He listened and nodded his head. Sometimes I had to ask him to repeat himself because I couldn't catch some of his words. He had an accent, not a heavy one but he spoke slightly differently from the other kids I knew.

Our conversation was interrupted by voices from the front room.

'Come on,' they shouted. 'We're waiting.'

We looked at each other and at the same time we leaned into each other. I could smell his aftershave. Our lips touched and I hesitated for a split second but then, eyes closed, pressed into his warmth. His lips were soft against mine.

Butterflies flittered through my tummy. We stayed locked together for what seemed like ages but was probably just a few seconds. When we pulled apart I was shaking slightly. I looked to the ground, suddenly shy and embarrassed.

'We'd better go back,' said Pat.

He was the first boy I ever kissed and sometimes I can still feel that first contact between us. When we walked back into the room we got a round of applause.

# 7

## Strange New World

The wind whipped up dust and made my eyes sting as I turned off the main road and started to walk to the industrial site. Lorries trundled past with full skips loaded on their flatbeds and waste paper blew from them into the air. Directly ahead of me was the dirty, muddy entrance to the yard where the lorries unloaded and the rumble of heavy machinery filled my ears.

I walked down a cul-de-sac at the back of town where few people went. On one side the backs of a row of offices gave way to derelict warehouses and once past the skip yard, there was a high white wall. Behind it I could just make out the roofs of some low buildings.

I was going to meet Pat at his home, a trailer park. It was the first time I had ever ventured into such a place and plenty of friends had warned me.

'They've got dogs there,' they said. 'Huge Rott-weilers and pit bulls and they'll attack you if they are not chained up. It'll be filthy, they'll be kids running everywhere.'

I didn't know it at the time but my sense of inquisitiveness was about to lead me on new journey. I had decided to make an unannounced visit to see Pat. I had called him a few times and we'd spoken on the phone but I was curious and I wanted to see where he lived.

Even the phone calls had been strange. The first time I called his mum had answered.

'Can I speak to Pat?' I asked.

'Which Pat?' she replied. 'Big Pat or Little Pat?'

'I'm not sure,' I answered. 'Your son, I think.'

'That'll be Little Pat,' she laughed. I didn't realise at the time that his family didn't call him Pat, they called him Brother.

I didn't know what to expect from the site but I suspected the tales of killer dogs and feral children were exaggerated, and I was curious – I wanted to see what a gypsy site looked like for myself. However, the talk had been enough to make me nervous. In fact, none of my friends had ever been on a traveller site either so none of them knew what to expect. No one I knew had, except the travellers themselves. I knew there would be trailers (travellers don't call them caravans) and possibly some holiday-style chalets, but that was all. Anything else was a mystery.

Although the traveller kids in town were happy to come to non-traveller clubs and the traveller men drank in some of the town's pubs, the integration did not appear to go the other way. At home they lived in a closed community, often in gated sites. I didn't know whether this was because they wanted to keep out gorgers – what gypsies call non-travelling folk – or to keep themselves locked in.

By the time I was approaching the entrance I felt apprehensive about what I would find and wondered whether I would be welcomed.

I called Pat my boyfriend but really we were both too young to know what the term really meant. First and fore-most we were friends and had started to hang out together. Pat had been round to my place a few times already, and – as I was curious about his way of life – I wanted to see where he lived, so I could see for myself what life as a traveller was like.

As I reached the threshold of the site I peered round the corner into a secret world. I could hear a dog barking in the distance but it was more of a yapping noise so I concluded it was unlikely to be a bloodthirsty pit bull.

There were no children on the site; in fact, it looked empty. I took in my surroundings. Laid out in neat rows around the central courtyard were around 15 trailers and chalets. Another chalet was being built beside the gates. Its breezeblock walls were already half finished. At one end of the site there was a brightly painted bungalow with the words *Jesus saves* painted over the arch of the front door.

The trailers were different styles and sizes. Some looked just big enough for two while others seemed more like the family mobile homes I had stayed in on holidays.

Next to each caravan and chalet there was a brick outhouse, each one about the size of a garden shed. Washing was drying on lines by most of them. I couldn't hear any voices or see any people, just the sound of that one dog and the rumble of machinery from the yard next door.

As I walked down to where Pat had told me he lived I looked inside some of the trailers I passed. What struck me was how neat and tidy they all were. Every one of the homes looked comfy and most of them had ornaments and crockery proudly displayed on shelves and tables. The windows were all clean and so were the curtains. Most had televisions and I could see a few screens flickering with daytime TV as I walked past.

As I looked through one of the windows of a trailer near the site entrance I jumped as a woman's face popped up and looked out. I felt embarrassed at having been caught gawping into her home but her face creased into a warm smile and she waved at me. She had gorgeous long, dark hair and looked young and friendly. I later learned she was Pat's mum, Karen. It was unusual for an unaccompanied non-traveller girl to be wandering on the site but I had spoken to her on the phone so she knew her son was friends with a girl.

About halfway down the row that backed on to the railway line, I saw a door open and Pat stepped out. He shared a trailer with his younger brothers, John Thomas and Levi. He was wearing jeans and a tight T-shirt and he came over, said hello, and led me out of the site.

'What do you think?' he asked.

'It's mad,' I said. 'They're nice, but they're so small. How do people live in them? How do you get a whole family in one?'

Pat explained that much of the time, gypsies lived communally, and that extended families shared and would own different trailers. So when he and his brothers were young they lived with his parents in one trailer but as they got older they moved to another, which was where he was now living. The men of the site were usually out working all day so it never seemed crowded.

My first venture on to a traveller site was over within minutes but I had been there long enough to realise that most of the rumours I had heard were unfounded. It looked like any other normal road, only with smaller homes.

As the months went by we became closer. I rarely went to the site again but Pat would spend time at my house. My mum liked him and so did my brother Brian. Dean reserved judgement. He was always protective of me. Pat would come round and have tea with us and we would watch movies together. Often we'd go to the cinema or to McDonald's and most days would meet up after school.

Being with Pat made me happy. More than anything he was fun to be around. He would always be dreaming up some new silly way to pass the time. We discovered a mutual appreciation of Kinder chocolate bars and one day Pat turned up at my house with a whole stack of them and a challenge.

'Let's see who can eat the most,' he said.

'You're on,' I laughed.

We sat on the floor stuffing bar after bar into our mouths, laughing so hard that it wasn't long before melted chocolate was dribbling down our chins. We were kids having fun.

But while life with my new traveller friend was always enjoyable, things at school were getting serious. My attitude and behaviour was going from bad to worse. I often felt I was being singled out because I had a reputation as a troublemaker. I reckoned that the teachers were look-ing for ways to catch me out. One day when I wore Ugg boots to school like so many of the other girls I was the one who was picked out of the playground and told to take them off.

I'd developed a chip on my shoulder and a fast tongue and was forever being reprimanded for answering back.

'Take that slap off,' a short-haired teacher ordered one day, gesturing at my face.

'Slappers wear slap, I wear make-up,' I spat back.

'Well, you look a slapper,' she said.

'At least I don't look like a lesbian,' I answered.

That little exchange led to Mum being called into the school – again. Mum scolded me afterwards but in the end had to agree with what I had said!

Things at home were going from bad to worse as well. I was arguing with Mum on a daily basis. I just had so much anger and spite in me that I would kick off at the smallest thing. To me it seemed like everyone was against me. Sometimes it felt like the only person who understood me was Pat.

But although we were getting closer, fate had other ideas. The strain of the arguments between me and Mum was getting too much and it was decided that I should go and live with Dad for a while. I still went to the same school but because Dad lived five miles away it meant I would be seeing much less of Pat.

I broke the news to him on Valentine's Day. On the way to meet him I stopped in a shop and bought him a teddy. It was sitting on the shelf and had beautiful smiling eyes, just like Pat's. It was fluffy and grey and was holding a red heart with the word 'LOVE' sewn into it. I gave the shopkeeper my money, put it in my bag and hurried to meet Pat.

He was waiting for me by the bus stop where we often met and we started walking together. Often we didn't have any destination or activity in mind, we just walked and talked, enjoying each other's company.

'I'm going away,' I told him. 'I don't know when I'll be back.'

'Where?' he asked. I could see he looked wounded.

I explained that my domestic arrangements were about to change and that I probably wouldn't be around as much as I had been. He understood and we made a pact that we'd stay in touch. We had each other's phone numbers and we could still text and whenever I was in town I would meet up with him.

Then I reached into my bag and pulled out the teddy bear.

'I got you this,' I said, handing him the gift.

He laughed. 'It's the best bear I've ever seen. I'll keep it always,' he promised.

After that we said our goodbyes and a few days later I went back to Dad's. We kept our promise initially and stayed in touch and sent each other text messages every day. But five miles is a long way when you're a pre-teen and you haven't got a car and the buses are infrequent. Over time we lost touch. I thought about Pat often but it just wasn't to be. It was the wrong time for us and besides, we were both still too young to know about romance and love. If anything, it was puppy love.

A while later I heard that Pat had also moved away. He'd gone to Scotland to work with an uncle. My gypsy boy was out of my life.

In hindsight maybe that did affect what happened next but at the time I wasn't given to self-analysis. We hadn't talked about the future or marriage, we were much too young for that. In those early teenage years boyfriends and girlfriends are lucky to last a few weeks, let alone for ever. Besides, there wasn't anything truly romantic between us at the time – more than anything else we were friends. Pat understood me. Perhaps having that under-standing, stable influence in my life was keeping me grounded and without it I was untethered, because soon after we lost touch I went completely off the rails.

It began with an argument in school. It must have been near the end of term because we were in class watching a DVD of the comedian Lee Evans. Perhaps I was mucking around or laughing louder than I should have been but halfway through the show I got chucked out of the classroom and told to stand in the corridor. I didn't go without giving the teacher some lip and by the time I got out of the room I was livid. Why was it always me? I was victimised and that was the one thing I vowed I would never be again. Not after the attack.

So when the teacher stood by the glass panel in the door with her back to me, that familiar angry red mist descended again and unthinkingly I punched the glass. It shattered with a loud crack and sharp shards flew across the room and showered her back. Then I reached through the empty window frame, grabbed her clothing and yanked her backwards.

The other kids in the class were screaming and the teacher was too shocked to say anything for a second. She wrestled herself away from me, opened the door and grabbed me.

I struggled with her but by then other teachers had come out of their classrooms, alerted by the shouts and the sound of breaking glass. I was taken to the headmaster's office for the last time.

I had been living on borrowed time for months and now they could no longer put up with criminal damage and assault. I was excluded with immediate effect. I walked out the gates and laughed. I hated school and I was glad I would never be going back. I had no idea what was going to happen to me from then on but for that brief moment in time I was free and it felt good.

# 8

# The Lowest Point

'Sit over there and be quiet.'

The teacher was stern and wasn't in the mood for any of my backchat.

A few days had passed since I had been thrown out of school and I found myself sitting back in a classroom again. I thought school was bad but this was much worse than what I had been used to. I was in a temporary education unit and my dreams of freedom were over before they had begun. I assumed that once you get thrown out of school, that's it. But the education system was not going to let me go that easily. Instead of being placed in another mainstream school or being home-schooled, I was in a parallel educational system, the place where the naughty children go while the authorities decide their fate. The unit I found myself in was school equivalent of limbo. The classroom was part of another set of civic buildings. There were around 20 of us there and we had one thing in common: the borough's schools refused to admit us. All of us had been expelled and we were in a transit centre. I started to realise how newly convicted prisoners felt while they waited to hear whether they were going to an easy open prison or to maximum-security jail.

The teachers in the temporary education units had seen it and heard it all before. They were trained to teach the worst of the worst; the kids everyone else had given up on. And so my attempts at riling them were swotted away like insignificant little flies. Without managing to get the reactions that I had been used to, I soon gave up trying. And even if I did get a reaction the kids with me were not impressed. Back in school I would get a buzz of appreciation when I said something or did something in class that got me a reprimand because as far as a lot of the pupils there were concerned, being a class rebel was cool. But in the place I was, they were all class rebels, we were all on an equal footing so no one was cooler than anyone else.

As the months passed I was shuffled between establishments. Haydock High refused to have me back and who could blame them? The reaction from my parents to my exclusion was a mix of disappointment and anger. Because I was out of the school system, I began to see less and less of my friends. Pat had gone and I began to feel abandoned and, without the audience of a classroom of impressed peers, I started to feel insignificant.

I became quieter as the weeks went on and more withdrawn. Even if there was a laugh to be had in class or a bit of mischief, more often than not I would take a back seat and let the others do the misbehaving. I became lethargic and withdrawn. I had no energy both in school and out of school. And at night, when I fell asleep, the demons of the past began to revisit me.

I would wake in the middle of the night in terror, disorientated and panting. Most nights my dreams took me back to the dark copse where the attack happened. The attacker, his face twisted and snarling, would be the last thing I saw before I woke, bathed in sweat. On waking it took a few minutes before I realised where I was and I sobbed into my pillow as my racing heart finally slowed.

I began to hate myself because I believed the attack was my fault and because my own stupidity had left me isolated from my friends. I felt like I was drifting aimlessly through life and sometimes my mood would be so black, I just couldn't see the point in carrying on.

I know now that I was probably clinically depressed but at the time all I felt was self-hatred and despondency. I had nothing to look forward to and nothing to aim for. I had no goals in life.

I had never been an ambitious girl. I didn't know what I wanted to do with my future. I didn't even believe I had a future. In the early years of secondary school I had wanted to become a model. I would look at magazines and see the beautiful women modelling clothes by designers such as Dior and Chanel and aspire to be like them. But it is not the kind of career choice that is encouraged in schools, probably for good reason, and so deep down I realised that it was more of a pipe dream than an achievable objective.

I was aimless and I had thrown away any chance I ever had of making something of my life by getting thrown out of school.

The black cloud that hung over me got darker and darker as time went on. I would find myself crying for no reason. I'd be walking home and suddenly would have an uncontrollable urge to weep. The sadness came in waves and almost knocked me off my feet at times.

I continued this descent into despair until one day something snapped. I don't know why it happened to be that particular day because at that point every day felt as hopeless as the next. But I woke once more in the early morning after yet another nightmare. Terrified and shaking, I lay in my bed and suddenly had an answer to all the misery.

'I'll kill myself,' I thought.

It was as though a light bulb had switched on in my head. Of course, what could be simpler? No more me, no more pain.

I got out of bed and padded quietly into the bathroom where I started to methodically check through the medicine cupboard. Along with the usual salves and ointments, there were cold medicines and painkillers. I grabbed a couple of boxes of paracetamol and took them to my room where I hid them. There was nowhere near enough to do the job properly so that day I stopped off in several chemists to buy packs of the drug. I reckoned I would need over 100 tablets to make sure I slipped into unconsciousness and never woke up again. I had never studied the effects of paracetamol and had no clinical experience whatsoever but I assumed 100 pills would be a big enough number to do the appropriate amount of damage needed to end my life.

That afternoon I returned home, went to my room with a bottle of water and my packets of painkillers and sat on my bed throwing handfuls of lozenge-shaped white pills into my mouth and washing them down with swigs of water. I was like a robot; I didn't think or feel anything. I was empty and all that mattered was getting as many pills into my system as possible. I wasn't crying, I don't even remember being sad. Sadness would have meant regret and I had no regrets about what I was doing.

The process took a long time and I stopped counting after 70. I was so full with water that I was struggling to swallow any more. When all the packets were empty I lay down on my bed and closed my eyes, wondering how long it would take before I passed out.

I thought of my family and wondered whether they would miss me. I thought about my funeral. I hadn't made any plans or written anything down. I hadn't even left a note. What good would that do anyway, no one cared. Then I thought about Pat and wondered if he would come to my funeral.

I drifted in and out of sleep, not sure whether it was my usual lethargy that was making me heavy-headed or the drugs. Then after an hour or so I began to feel the effects properly. At first I felt light-headed and woozy, almost drunk. Then the nausea began. My head started swimming and I began to experience that horrible feeling you get when you are drunk. The room spun and I battled to stop myself vomiting.

'Oh God, please make it stop,' I moaned as I squirmed on the bed to try and stop the awful see-saw motion in my head. Eventually I crawled on to the floor, hoping to find some stability there. At some point I must have passed out because I remember being woken up by vice-like stomach cramps ripping through my belly. I bent double in the foetal position and grabbed my tummy. I moaned and as I opened my mouth to vomit all that came out was white foam.

The pain intensified until wave after wave of agony finally battered me into submission. My breaths became shallow. The edges of my world softened and shadows crept in from the corners of my vision until everything went black. My attacker's face swam into view and dissolved. And then there was nothing.

In all I had taken 105 pills. I later learned that liver damage starts after 30 if the patient is not treated within 12 hours. It was a miracle I survived and my guardian angel came in an unexpected form: Brian, the brother who I'd spent so many years fighting with.

He was in the house while I was taking the pills and began to wonder what I was up to after I had been shut in my room for hours. He knocked a few times on my bedroom door and when I didn't answer he ventured into my room. And that's where he found me, sprawled on the floor, eyes rolled in the back of my head with white foam bubbling out of my open mouth.

He tried to rouse me and although I came to I was mumbling and incoherent. The ambulance was called and

I was rushed to A&E. The paramedics must have given me some sort of antidote on the way because I was conscious by the time I got to the hospital, and in the examination cubicle a nurse brought me a cup of disgusting-looking brown liquid.

'I'm not going to lie to you,' she said kindly, 'this will taste disgusting. But you need to drink it all and drink it down quickly. It will save your life.'

She explained that I needed to purge my system of whatever else was left in it and that this would help. She told me that paracetamol poisoning does not occur quickly. If it is not treated the consequence of taking too much of the painkiller can be liver damage and in the worst cases liver failure. Death is slow and painful. So slow, in fact, that some people who purposely overdose on paracetamol often have time to reconsider their actions and come to regret what they've done before they die.

I didn't want a slow, lingering death and so I raised the cup to my mouth and gulped down the liquid. The bitter, viscous fluid slid down my throat like thick tar. The nurse was right – it was disgusting.

I vomited after the first couple of mouthfuls. My stomach lurched in violent spasms as I gripped the side of the gurney I was sitting on. The nurse gently wiped my mouth and urged me to finish the medicine. I did.

I felt tender, damaged and raw as they sat me in a wheelchair and took me to a ward where I changed into a hospital-issue nightie and lay on the stiff sheets. One of the nurses on the ward came to bring me a drink of water.

'How are you feeling, love?' she asked.

I nodded mutely and rolled over. I didn't want to speak to anyone.

I fell into a dreamless sleep and wasn't aware of the constant vigil that the staff and my parents kept over me. I was on suicide watch and they checked me through the night to make sure I did not make any more attempts on my life. I couldn't have even if I'd wanted to; I was too exhausted.

The next morning when I woke up I felt groggy and slightly disorientated. It took a few minutes for me to realise where I was and what had happened. My tummy was aching from all the retching the day before, as if I had done hundreds of sit-ups. It was an effort to move. There was a drip in my arm. I couldn't remember how it had got there. I looked around the ward.

There were around eight beds, mainly occupied by teenagers. Many of them had obvious injuries like broken bones. A girl in a bed next to me had her leg in plaster. She caught me looking at her and smiled.

'What you in for?' she asked chirpily.

'Appendix,' I lied.

I didn't want anyone knowing my business, not because I was embarrassed about what I had attempted to do but because I didn't want to have to explain to people why I felt like I did and because I didn't want anyone's sympathy.

Later that day I overheard Mum and Dad talking about me when they thought I was asleep. They were worried and didn't know what to do or how to help me. I felt a pang of guilt as I listened to their hushed conversation.

Brian also came to visit.

'How you doing, sis?' he said in a mock cheerful voice.

'Why did you call the ambulance, Bri?' I accused.

'What?' He looked stung.

I jabbed my finger at him. 'You ruined everything, why did you have to come in my room and get involved?'

Brian just stared at me mutely. He couldn't understand my anger. He had saved my life after all. But at the time all I felt towards him was contempt. What nobody fully understood was that my overdose wasn't a cry for help. I really, truly wanted to die. If I had not been serious I would have taken 30 tablets, not over 100.

I was in hospital for three days in total and kept myself to myself. The doctors monitored me to make sure that there was no lasting damage to my liver and the nurses tried their best to cheer me up while they kept their watch over me.

I just felt empty and alone. The dark mood that had driven me to the edge of death had not lifted.

One day I was taken to see a specialist in a bright room at the back of the hospital. I wasn't sure at the time what she specialised in but I soon realised she wasn't a medical doctor. All she did was ask questions. Clearly she was a psychiatrist. She was kind and intense and started by asking questions about my family and my home life. At first it was easy enough but as the session progressed the questions got deeper. She wanted to know about my thoughts and feelings and ultimately she wanted to know why I did what I did.

I began to shut down. That protective mechanism I had developed, where I shut my darkest secret in a secure box at the back of my mind, kicked in and I became quiet and withdrawn. I wasn't going to tell anyone.

After I was released I went back to Dad's where I had been living. Dad was kind and caring and tried his best to give me the space he thought I needed but also kept a close eye on me. I was signed off schooling until I felt well enough to return.

The first time I went into the bathroom and locked the door I heard footsteps trudging up the stairs and along the hallway. Dad had come upstairs and I heard him walk into the next room and start going through the drawers.

'Just doing the washing, Sam,' he called out. 'You okay?'

I knew it was an excuse and that he was coming to check that I didn't do anything silly.

'I'm fine, Dad,' I called back.

He needn't have worried. Out of curiosity I pulled open the drawers of the medicine cabinet. They were empty. Even his razor had gone. They'd all been hidden away in case I made another suicide attempt.

Dad and Jamie tried to make me feel better and look after me. Dad would come and bring me breakfast in the morning and I knew he was keeping an eye on me.

A few days after coming home Dad drove me to a clinic where I had an appointment to speak to a counsellor. I had been adamant that I would not go. I vowed to myself that I wouldn't speak to anyone about my thoughts and feelings and ultimately why I tried to kill myself but I was cajoled and persuaded and in the end agreed to the appointment to keep everyone happy.

The plan was for me to go once a week, but even before I walked through the door for the first time I knew I would only go once. I have never been comfortable sharing my secrets with strangers.

The consulting room was cosy with two comfy chairs placed strategically at angles to each other so the patient – which was me – felt more comfortable. The counsellor, a middle-aged woman in casual trousers and a blouse, did not sit behind a desk as in most medical consultations. She was standing as I entered and smiled at me. Her eyes were warm and inquisitive.

'Hello, Sam,' she said, ushering me to the seat.

We both sat down and she began to flick through the file she had been holding.

'How are you feeling?' she asked.

I told her I was fine and waited quietly. She began to explain who she was and what she did. She told me that I shouldn't be embarrassed at all about telling her anything and that I did not have to talk to her about things I might feel uncomfortable talking about. She explained that whatever I spoke about was entirely confidential and would go no further than the room. She detailed her qualifications and explained that talking to her about what had happened and the reasons why would help me move forward in my life.

'There is no rush, Sam,' she said. 'I want this process to be helpful and for you to feel at ease.'

Over the next hour she asked me similar questions to the ones the psychiatrist had asked in the hospital. How did I feel? Did I still have suicidal thoughts? What were the most important relationships in my life? What made me angry? What made me sad?

I answered honestly but couldn't see the benefit of all this talking. And the questions got more personal: was there a specific reason why I took the pills? What had I been thinking about prior to the overdose? Was it planned or a spur-of-the-moment decision?

I walked away from the session drained, and told Dad that I wouldn't be going back. I did not want to confront the issues the lady was asking me about. I knew why I tried to kill myself: what good would it do me to discuss it with a stranger?

I bottled up my feelings and continued my life, staying mainly indoors and feeling miserable. Some days I couldn't even muster up the energy to get out of bed. Mum and Dad must have been frantic with worry but I didn't care. I just wanted to be left alone in my world of dark thoughts and depression.

During those weeks my friend Mel came to visit and we sat on my bed and chatted. My friends knew that I had taken an overdose and were supportive, although mainly they chose not to confront the issue. We were still all so young, what could they say that would make any difference or help in any way?

But Mel knew why I did it and was patient, caring and understanding as ever. She was very important to me, and although I had a big social circle, she was the closest friend I had. She was my confidante and knew what I was going through.

Having Mel to talk to lifted my mood. She had always been a happy-go-lucky, fun person to be around and her mood was infectious. Just having her around made me realise that not everything in my life was negative.

Slowly I began to venture out to spend some more time with friends. As the days went by I spent less time in my room and more time with family. I slowly started to reintegrate back into my surroundings.

At the time my little sister Tiffany was four and in those bleak weeks following my suicide attempt that I spent shut in my room, she would often come to try to cheer me up and pester me to play with her. One day, after I refused again, she walked away dejected and as I watched her walk out the door I suddenly realised that people cared about me, and that I was letting them down. I was being selfish and self-indulgent. We were never a family to wallow in our own misfortune, so what gave me the right to be so different?

I didn't want Tiffany to continually see me moping

around without any energy or motivation. She needed her older sis to be fun and playful.

'It's time to pull yourself together, Sam,' I told myself. I was ready to start living again.

# 9

## A New Beginning

The man sitting in front of me was trying to look stern and authoritative and was almost doing a good job but I could see a friendly glint in his eyes and no matter how hard he tried to be serious, he couldn't help smiling at me.

'Why would you want to do it, Sam?' he questioned. 'Think about it, what have you got to gain?'

I shrugged. 'I hate her, she hates me,' I replied simply. 'She gets on my nerves.'

He sighed quietly. 'Look, Sam, there are always going to be people in life who get on your nerves. You probably get on her nerves. If you go through life trying to batter the people you don't like, you are going to end up fighting all your life and you'll never get anywhere. What do you think would be the grown-up thing to do?'

'Walk away from it,' I replied.

'Why not be the bigger person and do that then?' he said.

I had picked myself up and made a vow that from now on things were going to change. But old habits die hard. I was back in the education system in a place called PACE. It was a centre for training and learning, a referral unit for kids with social, emotional and behavioural difficulties and the man speaking to me was one of the teachers, Eddie.

I had been caught arranging a fight with one of the other girls in the unit. We had never seen eye to eye and had decided to sort out our differences the best way we knew how – with our fists. It was all arranged. At three o'clock after lessons we would meet outside. But somehow Eddie had found out. Maybe there was a mole in the class – gossip always did seem to travel fast in the unit and the teachers were always one step ahead of the rest of us. They knew the signs and kept a watchful eye out for any possible problems.

I had packed up my books at the end of the day and had been heading outside for my pre-arranged meeting when Eddie called me back.

Agitated, I asked him what the problem was. He indicated for me to sit down and began to talk to me.

'I know where you're going and what you are going to do,' he said.

It wasn't an accusation, it was statement of fact. I tried to deny it at first and put on an act of injured innocence. But Eddie was no fool, none of the teachers in that place were.

He laughed. 'Come on, Sam, you haven't done anything, you're not in trouble. I just want a chat with you, that's all,' he said.

I knew there was no point being childish about it and denying what I was about to do, and I knew that he was right – I hadn't actually done anything wrong, yet, so I admitted the details to him. Rather than tell me off, Eddie talked to me like an adult. He didn't fly off the handle, he didn't reprimand me and he didn't judge me. He reasoned with me and let me have my say. Even though he was supposed to be the one in authority, it didn't feel like he was abusing his power over me. Instead I felt we were talking as equals.

I liked Eddie right from the time I started at PACE. He was nothing like the teachers I had met before. For one thing, he encouraged us to call him by his first name. And he dressed casually and spoke to us informally.

Eddie was tall with grey hair and always dressed very smartly. He spoke softly and never raised his voice, even when we started misbehaving. He made lessons interesting and wasn't condescending. And the other thing about Eddie that I liked and respected was that he always talked perfect sense. You couldn't argue with him because he was right about everything. Underneath his jovial banter, he was wise.

I knew that it would be silly to go outside the class-room that day and start a fight and deep down I knew I would not benefit from it in the slightest. It took Eddie to point that out to me, though.

'You've got a chance here, Sam,' he explained. 'It's up to you what you want to do with that chance, whether you want to take advantage of it or blow it.'

The decision was left up to me but explained in such a way that I knew there was really no decision at all. That afternoon, for the first time in as long as I could remem-ber, I walked away from trouble. And it was all thanks to Eddie.

PACE was an amazing place. The staff there did everything possible to make sure it felt welcoming and secure. Instead of the strict discipline of the temporary education unit I had been sent to after I was excluded, the teachers at PACE tried to bond with us, and spent time listening to us in an effort to understand where each of us was coming from. It must have been difficult for them because there were some challenging pupils there, but you could tell that each teacher had chosen to work in that environment because they cared and wanted to make a difference.

I felt at home there and slowly I began to respond to the staff's caring encouragement.

One of the huge differences in PACE as opposed to normal school was that we were rewarded for good behaviour. Most Fridays, the kids who had achieved things over the week were taken out on trips. We used to joke among ourselves that we were being rewarded for being naughty, and I am sure there will be people who disagree with the idea of treating excluded children, but the scheme worked.

Instead of the stick, we were offered the carrot and most of us responded well to it. The trips also helped with confidence and with team building. Despite a few grumbles we all got on well.

One of my favourite trips was rock climbing. We were taken to an artificial climbing wall in a mini-bus and strapped up with safety harnesses. I'd almost forgotten how sporty I used to be and the exhilaration of reaching the top of the wall, encouraged by Eddie and the other kids, gave me a huge sense of achievement. Standing on top looking down at their upturned faces below reminded me of what I used to feel like sitting on Vinnie's back all those years ago.

As the months went on the turmoil and rebellion that had ruled my life for so many years began to subside. It was as if a fog was slowly clearing in my mind and I started to feel positive about my future. When I think back to those days now I realise that the reason I responded so well to PACE and the way the system there was structured was because I was treated as an individual. I reacted to reasoning, not being told off and scolded. The teachers at PACE had time to talk to the pupils and time to try and work out how to motivate them and how to understand them.

By the time I left I was a different person. I still had issues to face but I was confident and hopeful.

After PACE I spent some months at another learning centre, Tamcos, where pupils were sent on work experience placements and at 15, I finally ended up at the college called Launchpad, which was where Pat had gone and prepared under-16s for the world of work after school. It was safe to say at that point that my academic career was not going to extend beyond my GCSEs, and at Launchpad we were taught core subjects such as English and maths and also trained in work-based skills and sent out on work-experience placements.

The range of courses on offer was vast and I learned how to plaster walls and lay bricks and secured work experience in a beauty salon in St Helens.

Sun and Beauty was a popular sunbed and beauty treatment salon with a mix of clientele ranging from youngsters like me, eager for a spray tan, to older women who used the sunbeds. I would help out around the place and book in clients. I tried as best as I could to be courteous and helpful. I enjoyed the work and was fascinated by all the beauty products and treatments on offer. I still harboured a secret desire to be a model and I loved to flick through the fashion and gossip mags, so it was intriguing to see how part of that industry functioned.

One of the highlights of my time at Launchpad was my first trip to London. We had been studying the play *Blood Brothers* as part of our English course but because none of us were particularly academic, the tutors were having trouble getting some of the pupils to read the script. So they came up with an idea.

'If we arrange a trip to see the play in the West End, will you all read it?' a teacher asked one day.

Everyone cheered and a few weeks later we headed on a train to London. It was an amazing day. I saw my first play and we had time after to visit the tourist attractions such as Trafalgar Square and Buckingham Palace.

Several months into my spell at Launchpad I was sent on another placement. I had to ask twice when I was told where I was going.

'A car body shop?' I said frowning. It didn't sound quite like the sedate female-focused beauty surroundings I had been used to.

'Yep, it's where they fix up cars that have been dented and scratched,' explained the tutor. 'They'll teach you all about bodywork, spraying, fixing dents...' He trailed off when he realised I was looking at him as if he was mad.

'I'll give it a go,' I shrugged.

The following morning I made my way to an industrial estate in St Helens and walked into P&B Moss car body repairs. I was a 15-year-old girl and nervous. I knew it would be full of men and was expecting all kinds of crude jibes and comments. I expected there would be posters of semi-naked women on the walls and it would be dirty, smelly and loud with loads of swearing.

Nervously I walked through the huge double doors of the workshop to find the man who was my contact, the owner Mark.

If there had been any posters on the walls they had been taken down that day and the man who came out to meet me was not the gruff, foul-mouthed stereotype I was expecting. Mark was friendly and enthusiastic and seemed happy to have me there. And the rest of the guys in the business were just as friendly. I'm not sure if they were on their best behaviour because there was a girl with them but I can't ever remember hearing them swear all the time I was there.

Mark showed me the ropes and over the first few days I shadowed him as he expertly prepared the cars for respraying, carefully masking the headlights and windows. I watched fascinated as the other lads took smashed and damaged vehicles and expertly bent them back into shape.

At college, when we learned bricklaying we always had to knock down what we had built and because I knew I would have to destroy my constructions, I never took much pride in what I was doing. Here in the body shop it was completely different. They were taking things that had been destroyed and building them back up again.

I enjoyed the whole process and within a few weeks Mark was letting me work on the cars myself. I carefully and meticulously prepared them for the sprayer, spending time on each one until I was 100 per cent sure it was ready.

Each morning I would get on the bus to travel in to work wearing my big baggy boiler suit and my steel toe-capped boots. Perhaps it was because of my tomboy past but I didn't feel uncomfortable dressed like a workman. Only my long hair gave away the fact that I was a girl. I rode the same bus that several of the pupils from Haydock High took and I knew some of them. Sometimes I would look at the girls in their short school skirts and listen to their conversations about school life and teachers and lessons. I realised that they were living in a completely different world from mine. I never felt regret; I didn't hanker after my schooldays. I was never cut out for school and, after all I'd been through, I was finally becoming happy within myself.

Things got even better when a familiar face arrived at Launchpad. Eddie had taken a job there and it was wonderful to see him again. We sat down during lunch one day and he was keen to know what I had been up to. I told him about the places I had been working and how much I enjoyed the bodywork placement and I could see that he was proud of me.

The pain that had led me to try and take my own life was receding further away and I was facing life with a renewed sense of enthusiasm. I was even getting good grades in my English class, thanks to my teacher Sarah.

Life for once seemed full of possibilities. The only thing missing was someone to share those possibilities with. After Pat I'd had no other boyfriends. I wasn't ready to have boys in my life and I wasn't looking. But they always say that you find the one you love when you least expect it and fate was about to reintroduce me to my gypsy boy... but he wasn't a boy any more: he'd turned into a man.

# 10

# Return of the Gypsy Boy

Even though Pat was no longer in my life, I often thought about him and wondered what had become of him. He had been one of my closest friends and the bond we shared when he was 14 and I was 11 was one of the most positive aspects of my short school years. By the time I was at Launchpad, things had become better between me and my mum, and I had moved back in with her. Back in my mum's home, I started to hang around our old haunts and that made me think even more about him. I heard his name mentioned a couple of times but what I heard was not nice.

'That traveller boy you used to hang around with has turned out bad,' a friend gossiped one day. 'He gets into trouble, he fights and drinks.'

It didn't sound like the sweet, considerate boy I used to know but perhaps people did change after all, I knew that more than most. I was sad when I heard the rumours because I knew deep down, whatever Pat had turned out to be, he had always had a good heart and he had always been good to me. Still, I made a note to be wary of him if I ever met him again.

It did not take long for me to find out for myself whether the rumours were true or not as, during my last few months at Launchpad, I ran into his brother.

It was a dull grey autumn afternoon in Earlestown and I was in the town centre with Amy, the girl I had fought with in the school playground all those years ago. I heard a familiar voice call my name from across the street. I looked over and saw John Thomas, strutting across the road with a group of his friends. He sauntered over to say hello. At that time I thought Pat was still in Scotland.

'What you up to?' John Thomas asked.

We began chatting and he asked how I was and where I had been.

'How's Pat getting on in Scotland?' I ventured. I prepared myself to hear all about how he'd been in and out of trouble but John Thomas looked at me and laughed.

'He's not in Scotland. He came back ages ago. He's living on the site and working.'

My heart skipped a beat. We were only five minutes' walk from the camp. I wondered if I should go in and see if he was there, but then I remembered the rumours.

We stayed with John Thomas, chatting about the town and work and people we knew, until the skies opened and it began pouring with rain.

'I'll walk you both home,' he offered as I huddled with Amy under a bus shelter to stay dry.

'Thanks,' I nodded, and the three of us set off in the direction of Amy's house.

We had walked about half a mile when I heard a vehicle slow down beside us and trundle along by the side of the pavement. I looked over and saw a white van with the windows misted by the downpour. I couldn't make out the driver's face inside the cab.

The window slowly wound down and a familiar face beamed out at me. Pat! I felt my tummy flip.

'Hi, Sam,' he smiled. 'I haven't seen you for years. What you doing out in this?' He held his hand out of the window to catch the raindrops.

'I was just on the way home,' I said to him. It was a shock to see him.

'You back with your mum then?' he asked.

I nodded, suddenly feeling guilty that I hadn't let him know I was back in town.

'Get in, I'll give you a lift,' he offered.

'Only if you take Amy first,' I said.

He happily agreed and Amy and I clambered into the

front seat of the van. John Thomas stood by the side of the road in the rain and Pat laughed, leaned across me to pull the door shut and drove off, leaving his brother drenched and alone.

As we drove to Amy's, I sneaked a look at Pat. The mischievous boy I remembered had grown into a tall, chiselled man. He had filled out and I could see his sinewy muscles straining under his tight T-shirt. His jaw was firmer than I remembered and the wispy moustache of his youth had been replaced by carefully trimmed designer stubble. He turned briefly and caught me looking. The eyes were still the same. The same sparkle danced in them. He smiled at me and I smiled back. Maybe he had turned into a moody troublemaker but at that point in his van, he certainly didn't look like one.

Within minutes we reached Amy's house and she thanked Pat and got out.

There was an awkward silence as we sat together, our thighs touching in the confines of the van. Pat gunned the engine and pointed the van back down the road towards my house.

'So, what you been up to?' he asked.

So much had happened in the years since we last met that I didn't know where to start. There was my exclusion from school, my overdose... not to mention the attack, but that had happened before I met Pat, although I was still experiencing its effects.

'Not much,' I shrugged.

Before long we were pulling into my road and Pat steered the van and parked in front of the house.

We sat awkwardly for a moment, listening to the rain drum on the metal roof.

'Well, I'd better go then,' I said. 'Thanks for the lift.' I opened the door.

Pat reached across and touched my arm. 'Remember that teddy, Sam?' he asked.

I nodded my head, recalling the Valentine's Day present from years ago.

'I've still got it,' he said. 'It's sitting at the end of my bed.'

'You liar,' I laughed.

'Seriously, Sam,' he said. 'I love that teddy; it reminds me of you. It's a shame we lost touch.'

I smiled at him. He had a sad look in his eyes, a distant longing.

'It's good to see you again, Pat,' I said as I climbed out the van. 'Thanks for the lift.'

I hurried up the path to the front door and walked in out of the rain. When I shut the door behind me I leaned against it and could feel my heart beating fast. I wasn't prepared for the emotions that were stirred up by seeing him again. He must have been thinking too, because it took several minutes before I heard the engine start and the van pull away slowly in the rain.

That night I lay in bed and thought about Pat. I had been totally unprepared for the way I felt when I saw him again. I hadn't realised how much I'd actually missed him over the years. He looked well and happy and I wondered whether the rumours about him had any truth to them or whether it was just anti-traveller prejudice.

The following morning I was on my way to the body shop when my phone buzzed in my pocket. I read the text. *Hi Sam, it's Pat. It was good to see you yesterday, can I take you out?*

How did he get my number? I had changed my phone since we last met. He must have got it from a mutual friend. I smiled to myself. He was so sweet, I thought, where was the harm? But then I stopped myself. What if the rumours were true? All I had done was sit in the van with him. I didn't really know anything about him.

I returned his text.

*Good to see you too, but am busy.*

I was confused. I hadn't ever had a proper boyfriend and I was totally inexperienced when it came to matters of the heart. I didn't want to get involved if it meant getting hurt.

But all that day at work I couldn't shake thoughts of Pat from my mind. And when I got home later that evening my phone rang. It was Pat.

'How was your day?' he asked.

'Fine, thanks, how was yours?' I answered.

We chatted for a while and again he asked me out the following night. I made an excuse about doing some chores for Mum and said goodbye. I could hear the dejection in his voice and felt guilty when I hung up.

He didn't seem so bad; what was stopping me?

Over the following days I discovered that Pat was not a quitter. He sent me several sweet texts and each time asked me to go out with him. Each time I made an excuse.

About two weeks after we first saw each other I was sitting indoors with Mum watching *Corrie* when the doorbell rang.

'I'll get it,' I offered, and jumped up from the sofa.

I opened the door and Pat was standing there with his trademark mischievous grin on his face and his hands behind his back.

'Hi, Sam,' he said. 'I wanted to show you something. Hope you don't mind me popping round.'

I had to giggle.

'What are you up to?' I asked with mock suspicion.

He reached out and presented something to me in the dark.

I couldn't see clearly and switched on the outdoor lights. My heart melted immediately. There, in his outstretched hands, was the grey teddy I had bought him all those years ago. And it was in pristine condition, as good as new.

'I told you I still had it,' he said.

'Aww, Pat,' I crooned. 'I didn't believe you. That's so sweet.'

I think he knew at that point his perseverance had paid off.

'So will you go out with me then?' he asked.

How could I refuse?

'Okay then,' I said in mock resignation.

Pat's face lit up. 'Great, I'll pick you up next Thursday. Cinema okay?'

I nodded and Pat skipped off up the path to his van. I watched as he pulled away with a smile on my face.

When I went back in the lounge Mum asked me who it was at the door.

'No one,' I replied, 'just someone trying to sell something.' I grinned to myself and settled back down to watch the telly.

\*

A few days later Pat arrived to take me on our first date. We had planned to go to the cinema, a safe choice for the first time in years that we would be alone together.

I spent ages choosing an outfit and wore jeans with a blue top. I teased my hair into curls and applied just the right amount of eye shadow, mascara and blusher and a liberal slick of lippy.

By the time he arrived my nerves were jangling. I like to think I am a good judge of character and from what I had seen so far, Pat was still the same person I had been close to when I was younger. The personality and the thoughtfulness were still there, he'd just grown up, and he had turned into a hunk.

He arrived wearing a tight T-shirt, jeans and a leather jacket and as he led me to the van he opened the door and helped me in.

We drove to the local multiplex and at every opportunity Pat opened doors and checked that I was happy and enjoying myself. I couldn't believe what a gentleman he was being. He wouldn't let me pay for anything and was attentive and good company.

After the film we drove to get something to eat and he asked all about the bodywork shop. He was genuinely interested in what I had to say and asked about my family. He remembered everyone.

By the time we were in the van and on the way to drop me off home, any apprehensions I had were long gone. The rumours were rubbish. He had changed on the outside – for the better – but underneath his heart was still the same: good, strong, caring and true.

'He's a catch,' I thought to myself.

He pulled up his van beside the kerb in front of my house and walked me to the front door.

'Thanks, Sam,' he said. 'I've had a great night.'

'So have I,' I replied.

We leaned towards each other and electricity sparked between our lips. I breathed him in as we had our first proper kiss and all the memories came flooding back of that awkward moment in the hallway years ago. It felt like I was home, in his arms, where I was meant to be.

When we pulled apart he fixed me with his deep eyes.

'Can I see you again?' he asked.

'Of course you can,' I smiled.

# 11

## In the Family

After that first night I had no more doubts. Right away we started seeing each other as boyfriend and girlfriend.

As far as I was concerned, we were just like any other teenage couple. At 18, Pat may have been a few years older than me but because of what I had been through, I had grown up quickly. Mentally we were on the same level.

We enjoyed the same things, listened to the same music and liked the same films. At heart I was an old-fashioned girl. I may have been a rebel at school but when it came to romance, I still believed in tradition. And Pat too was a traditional guy – a real gentleman in a world where that was very rare.

As we got to know each other I came to understand that Pat's chivalrous streak was not unusual for a traveller. I started to learn more about his way of life and his beliefs. Gypsy men look after their women as if they were made of precious metal. They see it as their duty to provide for their wives and many of them would be embarrassed and ashamed if their wives had to go out to work.

In traveller life, I discovered, the men earn the money and the women look after the home. In this, Pat wasn't as traditional as some other travellers and explained that as far as he was concerned, if a woman wanted to work then she should have the choice, but if she wanted to be a homemaker for her husband then the husband should be prepared to earn a decent living for them both.

Pat is a twenty-first-century traveller with all the old-school benefits. He believed that women should have choices and he believed in equality but he also believed in manners and treating women with respect.

And that suited me fine.

After our first date we became inseparable. I saw Pat almost every day. He met my mum, who of course remembered him from when he was younger, and depending on whether I was at work experience or college he would pick me up and come home with me for a while, then either go back to his family or take me out, usually for something to eat or to the pictures.

The pattern continued for weeks and I loved his company. On our days off we would go for walks in the park or hang around with friends.

But one thing kept niggling at me. Pat would always

come and pick me up and would always come to my house but, apart from the one time I had gone to meet him at his trailer when I was 11, I had never been to where he lived and the only person in his family I had ever met properly was his brother.

I confronted him about it one day when we were out.

'Tell me honestly Pat, are you embarrassed of me?'

He looked shocked.

'Of course not. How could I ever be embarrassed of you?'

I explained that although we had been together for nearly a month, I had never met his parents and had never seen where he lived. I told him I was worried that he was ashamed to introduce me to his family because I was not a traveller girl. Just as there are prejudices towards travellers from some non-travellers, there are also prejudices towards non-travellers from some travellers, and although I knew Pat was open-minded, I worried that his family might not accept me.

He reassured me and explained that there was no such bigotry in his family. While he understood why some gypsies were intent on trying to protect their way of life, which is dying out, he had grandparents who were non-travellers themselves and so his family did not discriminate in any way. They accepted people for who they were.

Me, aged three, before I refused to wear dresses.

Me and my brothers Dean and Brian being friendly to each other for once.

The biggest member of our family, Vinnie, and me.

This is me, aged 10, on holiday in Cyprus with Tiffany and Brian. It was the last summer of my childhood I'd enjoy.

The teddy bear I bought for Pat as a lasting reminder of me and our love.

On our way to John Patrick's christening – my first official outing in the traveller community.

Me and Pat tucking into some pie and gravy in the caravan. I felt so at home.

This was the day after Pat's brothers shaved off his eyebrows! I still think he looks gorgeous though.

This was taken on a night I'll never forget: New Year's Eve and the day Pat proposed to me.

All dressed up for one of my two hen parties. My pink tutu was a little hint of what I'd look like on my wedding day.

Pat and his brother John Thomas standing outside the Monster Truck that got him to the church.

© UNP

Me arriving at the church. My 20-stone dress meant it wasn't easy to get out of the Cinderella carriage.

My dress in all its glory! Thankfully, my mini-bride Tiffany was on hand to help me get around.

St Patrick's Church where my dream man Pat was waiting for me.

After a tiring walk, I eventually made it to the altar. Pat looked so handsome – a real Prince Charming.

My dutiful bridesmaids in their pink and black corsets. They looked amazing!

Signing the register. I was so excited I could barely hold my pen.

The newly married Mr and Mrs Lee! I was so pleased to be able to call Pat my husband.

© UNP

Pat could barely fit in the carriage with my dress. But it was still a dream come true.

1. Our wedding cake in the style of a fairy-tale castle. It tasted magical too!

2. Pat, me and my mum finally getting to sit down at the reception. Mum was so proud.

3. My mum-in-law Karen trying to get in close enough for a quick snap.

4. Pat getting in the party mood with bridesmaid Elysia.

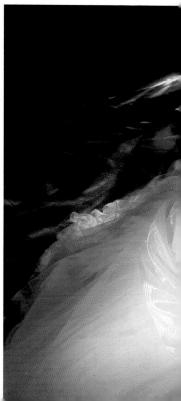

Our first dance and the moment my dress came alive.

The lights and butterflies were dazzling, but not as much as my dishy groom.

My dress almost took up the whole dance floor. I know here I was thinking about just how perfect my special day had been. It was everything I'd wanted it to be and more.

© PA

The day after our
wedding and Pat
and me could finally
be alone in our very
own caravan. This is
the dress I wore to
the fancy dress party
at the local.

Us at the BAFTA
Nominees party.
Man and wife and,
underneath my glam
dress, Baby Lee. We
can't wait to be a
mummy and daddy.
I guess fairy-tales
really do exist!

Then he sighed and tried to tell me about gypsy court-ing tradition, which was a bit of an eye opener for me. I had never even heard the term 'courting' until we started to go out together.

'When a traveller meets a girl that he is serious about, he won't just take her home and introduce her to his whole family. It is disrespectful. I couldn't just take you back to the site, it wouldn't be right. There is a traditional way of doing things. Before you meet anyone, you need to meet my mum,' he said.

He explained that normally a gypsy boy would tell his mother that he had found a girl and he would take her to meet his mum, almost like a job interview. Only once the mum was satisfied that the girl was suitable could she be introduced to the rest of the family.

I wasn't sure how I'd get to meet Pat's mum but found out a few days later when I was at home and my phone rang. Pat's name flashed up on the display.

'Hiya,' I answered.

But it wasn't Pat's voice. It was a woman.

'Is that Sam?' she asked. She sounded friendly.

'Yes, who's this?' I answered.

'It's Pat's mum, Karen. I was just passing with my daughter Chantelle and thought I'd pop in and say hello.'

It was the last thing I was expecting but she sounded so warm, not at all scary.

'Of course,' I said and told her my address.

Within a few minutes the doorbell rang. I didn't even have time to get nervous. I called out to Mum to tell her we had visitors and opened the door.

Pat's mum Karen was standing on the doorstep. I vaguely recognised her from when I had visited Pat at the trailer site four years ago – she was the woman who had waved at me out of her window. She had long, shiny, dark hair and looked young, slim and attractive. She had Pat's sparkling eyes and a broad smile on her face. Standing next to her was Chantelle, Pat's sister. She looked like a younger version of her mum, dressed immaculately with flowing dark locks.

'Hello, Mrs Lee,' I said. 'Come in.'

Pat's mum apologised for turning up at such short notice and said, 'I wanted to see who it was who has been making my boy so happy.'

I blushed and lowered my head shyly.

Pat had told his mum all about me and in true traveller tradition she wanted to meet me and see what I was like. In a way I suppose she was coming around to check me out, but it certainly didn't feel like I was being tested and it showed how much she cared about her son. I did, however, make sure I was polite and didn't swear.

Karen obviously didn't want Pat mixing with the wrong type of girl and I would imagine that had I not met with her approval, our relationship would have been nipped in the bud. Although traveller wives are expected to serve their husbands faithfully, they also hold the balance of power in the marriage and the family. Relationships rarely flourish without their consent.

For the next hour Karen, Chantelle, Mum and I sat in the kitchen drinking coffee and chatting. Karen asked me all about college and work and talked about Pat, what he was like as a child and how much he liked me.

A little while later Pat arrived and sat with us. I noticed approving glances pass between him and his mum and realised that I was getting the seal of approval that he desperately wanted from his family. Chantelle was lovely too; she spoke about her son and motherhood.

When they went Karen turned to me and gave me a hug.

'You know, Sam, you are welcome to come to the site any time you want.'

'Thank you,' I smiled, 'that's good to know.'

I waved them off as they went and realised that was it, it seemed that I had won over Pat's mum. I was smiling to myself as I walked back into the kitchen to help Mum clear away the cups.

Later that night Pat called.

'She loves you,' he said. 'I knew she would, she thinks you're great.'

Some people think that traveller communities are hostile and closed, that they keep themselves to themselves and do not mix freely with strangers. To a degree that is correct. Many travellers are wary of the wider community just like non-travellers are wary of travellers. But they are not unwelcoming; they are a little more choosy about who they let into their world. Before I met Pat I probably would have thought from the way people spoke about them that they would not like non-travellers entering their community. But that was not my experience. I was welcomed and discovered that once you are accepted they are the most hospitable people you could meet. Of course there are a few bad apples, that's true of all walks of life. With Pat's mum's approval I was welcomed into the family with open arms.

The next day Pat picked me up and drove me to the site where he lived. I had been invited round for tea with his family. The camp had hardly changed since the last time I visited four years before. The trailers were still lined in neat rows and the television screens were still flickering in the windows.

I was nervous about going into Pat's mum's home for the first time and told him so.

He laughed. 'Don't be daft, babe,' he said. 'She's been looking forward to seeing you all day.'

As we pulled up, the door was flung open and Karen stood there, framed by the warm light from inside beckoning us in.

The smell of home-cooked food wafted out as we stepped up into the living area.

The shelves and walls were festooned with expensive-looking plates and crystal ornaments and the table had been laid out with fine china.

'Make yourself at home,' Karen said as she dished up a dinner of meat stew and vegetables from a slow cooker on the kitchen work surface.

She explained that slow cookers were invaluable to traveller wives because they took up little room and you could prepare almost anything in them.

The food was delicious and we were joined for dinner by the rest of Pat's family: Chantelle, John Thomas and his little brother Levi. Pat's gran also lived on the site, as did two of his aunts. I later learned that travellers call other older travellers aunts and uncles even if they are not blood relatives and that all travellers of the same age are cousins. I was once on the phone to Pat and he began talking to another guy who he'd met in the shop he was in.

'That's my cousin,' he told me.

'What's his name?' I asked.

'I don't know,' replied Pat.

Back on the site Pat explained to me that even though we were now officially a couple in his mother's eyes, I was not allowed to go into his trailer where he lived with his brothers as this would be seen as inappropriate, even if his brothers were in there with him. In fact, it would be frowned upon if Pat and I spent time alone anywhere other than perhaps out of necessity when we were in the van driving to and from places. This meant that our courting had to take place in public: at cinemas, in restaurants and parks. There would be no locking ourselves away privately and as far as I was concerned that would be a good thing. I was still only 15 and my feelings for Pat were pure.

From then on Karen became a big part of my life. I would see her almost daily and I'd pop in for a cup of tea and a chat and to see if I could help with anything whenever I was nearby. I soon learned that gypsy women helped each other with the housework, chores and childcare and wanted to observe their rules when I was on their site.

Karen in turn would often take me shopping. I could see where Pat got his manners from because she too always asked first.

She would call me up when I was at college and ask, 'Can I take you shopping later?'

Of course, I was only too happy to go. She was lovely company and had a kind, caring streak that I warmed to immediately.

The first time she took me out on her own we went to St Helens to look around and she showed me clothes shops I had never seen before: stores and boutiques with amazing dresses and designer gear that had eye-watering price tags on them. She explained that traveller girls do not go out on their own unless they go to family functions like weddings and christenings and when they do they like to dress up and make a statement. Many of them will have outfits made for special events and the more intricate and stunning the better. I loved the idea of dressing to impress and rifled longingly through the racks of brightly coloured outfits. It seemed that gypsy girls didn't do understated colours or styles.

A whole new world was opening up to me and I was learning new things every day.

Meanwhile, my time at college came to an end and, after encouragement from Eddie and my English teacher

Sarah, I passed my GCSE in English. I still had no idea
what I wanted to do for a living and for a while went
back to do some more work experience at the car bodywork shop.

After a few months though, I knew I had to get a job
that paid me a proper wage and applied to work in the
local bakery. It wasn't what I'd planned to do for a career
but I had never been the career type and with an academic
record like mine my options were limited. So when the
job was offered I accepted gratefully and took possession
of an orange Greggs T-shirt and black baker's hat.

I worked very long hours. We had to start early in the
morning as the bread was baked on-site and although at
first the smell of warm fresh bread made my mouth water,
by the middle of most afternoons I wouldn't have cared if
I never set eyes on another bap again. However, it was
good to have a purpose and to be earning my own money,
even if the wage packet was not massive.

On dates I would always take money with me and try
to pay my way, but Pat would never accept. It was a
mixture of old-fashioned manners and gypsy pride and
even though he was supportive of me working, he didn't
want to take the money I earned.

It often led to stand-offs and arguments. On some
occasions I was desperate to contribute at least a little

something, but Pat wouldn't budge. Matters came to a head in the cinema one day (by then the staff there knew us on a first name basis because it was one of the places we could court in and subsequently we went sometimes two or three times a week). On that particular day, as we had gone in Pat had dashed off to the loo. Seeing a rare opportunity I went to the counter and bought our tickets. I actually felt bad while I was doing it because I knew how traditional Pat was and I felt a little sneaky. When he came back out and started queuing for the tickets I told him not to bother because for once it was my treat. I wanted to show him how much I appreciated him.

Pat looked at me and shook his head. 'I'm paying,' he insisted, 'here, take the money.'

He tried to put £20 in my hand but I refused. So then he tried to shove it in my pocket and, when that didn't work, in my bag. He was starting to get agitated but I decided to make a stand.

'Pat, I'm not taking it,' I told him, stamping my feet in frustration. 'You pay for everything all the time, tonight it's my turn.'

Pat crossed his arms. 'Fine then, if you won't take the money I won't watch the film.'

And he stood there, daring my next move.

'Okay,' I said, sitting on a nearby seat, 'neither of us will see it.'

It was a Mexican stand-off, a game of chicken over two cinema tickets. The clocked ticked down, the crowds disappeared into the cinema and we remained outside. The film started; we could hear the opening credits.

After ten minutes he won. Exasperated I gave in and took the money, just to save wasting two tickets. Pat smiled; he'd made his point.

The weeks rolled by and Christmas came round quickly. It was our first one as a couple and as my mum was having Brian and Dean over, I decided to spend part of the day with her and part of the day with Pat and what had now become my other family.

Christmas on the trailer site was a fun, friendly affair. Many travellers are deeply religious: the ones with Irish roots are devout Catholics and the others are Church of England, so Christmas and Easter are important times of the year.

On the site Pat's family had a traditional turkey dinner just like my family did, but that was where the similarity ended. The people on the site wandered in and out of each other's trailers to spread Christmas cheer; it was like an all-day party and everyone helped each other. No one was left on their own and I thought back to when Mum and

Dad had split up and some of the lonely Christmases she had endured.

Pat took me aside and gave me the carefully wrapped gifts he had bought for me. Excitedly I tore off the paper. He'd bought me a Calvin Klein and a Kylie Minogue fragrance gift set. I hugged him and we shared a quick kiss under the mistletoe before I presented him with my gift – a Liverpool football shirt. Pat is a huge fan and loved the gift. He slipped it straight on over his sweatshirt and I rarely saw him without it on over the next few weeks.

While Pat's family accepted me with open arms, the same wasn't always true of my family. Although Mum and Dad and Brian liked Pat, Dean had reservations. Perhaps he was protective of his little sis, perhaps it was because Pat was a gypsy, but he was unsure of the new man in my life and was not thrilled when I told him Pat was a traveller.

Pat was desperate to be accepted and decided that the only way Dean would be able to see how good he was for me was if they met properly, man to man. When he told me his plan I was nervous.

What if Dean decided he didn't like Pat, what if they got into a fight? Then I looked at Pat and saw the concerned look on his face and realised something: how could anyone not like Pat?

So the next time I was at Dad's, and Dean, who lived with his partner Becky at the time, was there, Pat came round and knocked on the door. I let him in and showed him into the living room where Dean was watching telly. I stood nervously in the doorway as I watched my boyfriend and my brother size each other up. Dean shook his hand warily and Pat made a suggestion.

'Let's go for a pint?' he offered.

Dean nodded and the two lads disappeared down the road, leaving me sitting cross-legged on the sofa biting my nails and imagining them both punching each other's lights out in an alleyway somewhere.

After two hours had gone by I was even more concerned and so when I heard a key in the lock I sprang to my feet and ran into the hall.

'Where have you b—' I started to say, and then stopped.

Pat and Dean were standing in the hall swaying against each other, their eyes bleary and red. In mumbled sentences they explained that one pint had led to two, then three and then they'd lost count. They both laughed. Dean had finally realised that Pat wasn't such a bad lad after all.

# 12

## Falling Deeper

The traffic was backed up along the M62 and we crawled along in the slow lane, bored and hot.

'Why do we have to go all the way to Manchester?' I moaned, staring out the window.

'Don't worry, Princess, it'll be worth it,' assured Pat with a cheeky grin.

I didn't know where we were going; it was a surprise. All I knew was that Pat was taking me somewhere special.

We were off on another of his adventures. He'd often pick me up and pretend to have no idea where we were going, then suddenly we'd 'happen' upon an amusement park or a bowling alley.

The week before our mystery Manchester trip he had pretended to get lost driving around St Helens. I knew it was one of his tricks because he drove around the area every day for work but I played along. Then, after half an hour, he pulled into the car park of a leisure park and I

~ 119 ~

saw the signs for crazy golf. He'd planned it along and we spent a fun afternoon tapping golf balls through miniature windmills.

So even though it was a drag being caught in the traffic, I had a sneaky suspicion there would be something exciting waiting for us at wherever the ultimate destination was.

We eventually pulled up at the side of a nondescript main road in the inner city.

Pat parked the van, turned to me and laughed.

'Welcome to Cheater Mill,' he said, hopping from the van and running round to open the door for me.

I couldn't see any signs saying *Cheater Mill* but noticed a street sign that read *Cheetham Hill*. I soon found out why Pat had given it an alternative title.

It looked like any other slightly run-down, out-of-the-city-centre shopping street. It was busy with shoppers, though. There looked to be several other travellers walking around. By now I had become good at picking out travellers from a crowd: the boys wore designer T-shirts and had their hair short, spiky and gelled, and the girls – who, more often than not, wore their dark hair long – were usually in short skirts and cropped tops. I was reminded of the first time I went shopping with my mum in TopShop – I was now used to what had seemed like an alien environment then, but this was something else entirely – almost like a universe that existed separately, but parallel, to my own.

I was intrigued because as we ventured down the street I didn't recognise any of the shop names. There were no high street brands like Next or River Island. Instead, many of the stores were Asian. Mainly they sold clothes and accessories, and as we started to look closely I noticed a lot of designer names – Gucci, Prada, Chanel. There were T-shirts, bags and shoes. I picked up a Dior clutch bag and turned it over in my hands.

The label looked authentic, the stitching was straight and as far as I could tell the leather was decent quality. But instead of the £400 price tag that I had been expecting, the bag cost £30.

'You'll get it for much less than that,' winked Pat. 'And anyway, the good stuff is out the back.'

The penny dropped.

Cheater Mill was where people went to get their fake designer gear. Everyone I knew loved labels and I was no exception. I couldn't afford the real thing so when the opportunity came up to buy fake goods in a market or from a hawker in one of the pubs, I would be first in line. I loved my fake Ugg boots and they probably lasted longer than the real things. It was that demand for cheap counterfeit designer gear that meant on a Saturday afternoon, Cheater Mill was doing a roaring trade.

In the first shop we ventured into, Pat wandered off and came back a minute later with the storeowner who ushered us to the back of a building. He unlocked a door and waved us through. We walked into what appeared to be another shop – a shop within a shop. It was bizarre. The racks and walls were decorated with the same colours as the shop at the front but the difference was the goods on sale. There were clothes of every label you could think of: Hugo Boss, Armani, Ed Hardy. Some were quite obviously fake, with ironed-on badges, but others you couldn't tell the difference.

And it was same in many of the stores. In one we were shown into a basement full of people rifling through counters and shelves filled with clothes and accessories. In another a man took us upstairs and opened a cupboard full of watches. The names leapt out: Rolex, Breitling, Tag, Cartier. I was reminded of when Harry Potter first discovers the secret world of Diagon Alley. Like him, I had stumbled on a magical hidden high street where nothing was what it first appeared.

In one shop, some Chanel bedding caught my eye and I picked it up to pay for it.

Pat stopped me. 'I'll do it,' he said, taking the pack from me.

I had come to realise that Pat was an expert negotiator. He would rarely pay full price for things and believed that you could get a discount on most things, if you tried and if you had the charm to go along with it.

He was forever trying his luck at McDonald's because I usually had a burger with no bun and no tomato. Pat would reason with the staff that a burger without all the advertised ingredients costs less to make, so in turn should cost less to buy. You couldn't argue with his logic but still the managers at the fast food chain were unmoved.

When it came to my Chanel bedding he offered the man behind the counter less than half the price advertised on the tag. The man shook his head and for the next ten minutes they bartered with each other until they agreed on a price and shook on it. Pat did the same a few shops later with an Ed Hardy T-shirt.

Travellers will usually try and bargain for certain goods in certain shops. They won't try and get a reduction off the daily newspaper in Tesco but in independent shops for bigger value goods they will try to haggle. And they are not obsessed with talking about money. For obvious reasons they are not concerned with house prices and they rarely discuss what they earn with outsiders. But they are not secretive for the sake of it. They see it as disrespectful to ask about money and they don't value money in itself; they value their possessions and the things money can buy. There is also some truth in the fact that, if people know how much a shop is willing to discount for certain items, and too many people ask for that discount, the shop eventually stops giving the discount and no one benefits.

And so out of respect I would not divulge what we paid in Cheater Mill but what I would say is that we walked away with bags full of designer gear and still had change from £200.

Despite the custom of haggling, traveller life is not always about saving money. For the right occasions and events, traveller women will spend small fortunes. Weddings and christenings are always a big deal in any traveller family calendar, as I was to see during my first traveller function, which was the christening of Chantelle's son, John Patrick.

Young unmarried traveller girls are shielded from wider society and not encouraged to go out on their own so the only places they get to meet other travellers, and more importantly traveller boys, are family events. And because of this, they make a real effort to stand out. I had seen wedding pictures and videos from events Pat and his family had been to in the past. The girls were spray-tanned and manicured to perfection with awe-inspiring outfits, many of which revealed plenty of bronzed flesh. I wanted to look as good as some of the girls I had seen.

There were no real rules. Many people might say some of the outfits were outrageous or tacky. I disagree. I think that if you only get to go out socially on rare occasions, as many gypsy girls do, why not make an effort?

So John Patrick's christening presented me with a dilemma. I rifled through my wardrobe at home and there just didn't seem to be anything that was suitable, or different enough.

I spoke to Pat about my concerns. 'I don't want to look out of place,' I said.

Bizarrely, dressing plainly would have marked me out as an outsider. I was acutely aware that I would probably be the only non-traveller at the event and I was nervous. Pat's family were lovely of course and I got on with them all but there would be plenty of people there I didn't know and I wanted to blend in. I worried that because I was a non-traveller I might get singled out.

'We'll get you something made,' said Pat.

'That'll cost a fortune,' I gasped.

But Pat was adamant. He explained that at traveller events the girls compete with each other to wear the most striking outfits. I could go wearing high street clothes and no one would say anything, but the idea was to try and stand out from the crowd. It was not a bitchy competition but most girls understood that in order to make an impression, they needed to look individual and striking.

So at Pat's suggestion I sat down with Chantelle and we begun to sketch some details of what kind of dress I could wear. Many traveller girls will do the same thing before any event. Sometimes they even save images from the Internet of outfits they like on their phones to take with them when they go to the dressmakers. They will have a folder of sketches and photos cut from magazines. Many will design their own wedding dresses when they are little girls and keep the designs until they are ready to get married.

For my christening party dress I got inspiration from the can-can-style dresses in the movie *Moulin Rouge*. Chantelle carefully drew out a corset-style top attached to a frilly dress which was higher at the front than the back to show off my legs. I chose black and shocking pink as the colour scheme and Pat took the design to a dressmaker in St Helens along with my measurements.

In all the outfit cost around £300 but when I collected it and tried it on, it was worth every penny. I gasped when I looked at myself in the mirror. I looked like a cross between a Parisian burlesque dancer and a Wild West saloon girl; I looked and felt like a movie star and I knew there would be no one else in the world with the same dress. I loved it.

On the day of the christening my nerves were jangling. It was my first big test in the wider traveller community but I felt a little better knowing that in my dress designed to stand out, I would fit right in. I chose a dainty silver necklace and matching earrings and finished the outfit off with silver strappy heels.

Pat wore a sleeveless blue tight-fitting vest and dark trousers, as it is just as common for traveller men to wear casual outfits to functions as it is for them to wear suits.

By the time we arrived at the venue I was jittery and anxious. What if no one liked me? Another traveller tradition I had learnt was that women should not smoke in front of the older men and because there were older traveller men there, I knew I would not be able to calm my nerves with a sneaky cigarette. Pat smokes, but will not smoke in front of his father out of respect, and he had told me about traveller men in their thirties and forties who did not smoke in front of elders… even if the elders were smokers themselves.

'Don't worry, babe,' Pat assured me as we walked into the venue. 'I'll be with you.'

'Don't leave me on my own,' I begged.

The post-christening family gathering was taking place in a community centre and Pat's mum beckoned me over to sit with her and Chantelle. Pat squeezed my arm and off I went.

We chatted and as time wore on I realised that Pat had disappeared along with all the other men. I got up to find him and discovered he was in a room with the rest of the male guests, drinking and laughing. I felt hugely self-conscious when I walked in because I was the only female there. Pat saw me and walked over, then guided me out to talk in the hallway.

'You said you wouldn't leave me,' I whined.

'I've got to stay in here with the men, it's how things are done,' he tried to explain.

'But you're supposed to be with me,' I said, getting angry.

Pat explained that at most gypsy functions the men and women will not mix and sometimes go off into sepa-rate rooms.

'Don't worry, you'll get used to it,' he tried to reassure me. 'Mum and Chantelle will look after you.'

But it was unfair to expect them to babysit me all after-noon and I told Pat I wanted to go. We went into the car park where we continued to row. I felt that Pat had aban-doned me and he felt that I should just try and enjoy myself.

Our voices got louder and louder and in the end we were both so annoyed with each other that we left and didn't speak a word on the way home. My initiation into the traveller community had been a disaster and when he pulled up outside my house to drop me off I climbed out, slammed the van door and stomped off.

Our tiff did not last long, though. He came round the next morning with flowers and we made up. After that day, we came to a compromise when we attended any future traveller events. I got used to the male and female divide and accepted that was part of the tradition, and Pat accepted that I was sometimes insecure when I did not know lots of people and would come and check on me at regular intervals.

Another thing I discovered about traveller functions was that it was not only the older girls who got dressed up. Some of the most amazing outfits were worn by the little girls, the five- to ten-year-olds. They would wear skin-tight Lycra leggings and tight cropped tops, tiny short skirts and heels. They would get made up with hair extensions and blusher and lipstick, and even six-year-olds had spray-tans!

At christenings the christening gowns would often be made to order and some I had heard about were as big and extravagant as wedding dresses.

Many non-travellers frown at this tradition. They believe it makes the girls look too grown up but I think that attitude is just snobbery. What little girl doesn't want to look like her favourite pop star or hasn't, at some point, gone through her mum's make-up drawer? It was all part of growing up, and the difference with young traveller girls is that they don't get many opportunities to express themselves by dressing up, so when they do, they are encouraged to go for it. No one in the traveller community bats an eyelid when an eight-year-old in a Lycra catsuit gyrates to a Beyoncé song at a wedding; it's judgemental non-travellers who had the problem.

And that's because most non-travellers are unaware of just how moral and sheltered the life of a traveller girl was. The young ones rarely left the site unless with family or for school and because functions like weddings and christenings are safe environments, they can dress up in whatever style or fashion they choose.

You did not see traveller girls hanging around the streets, they were kept on site and expected to help their mothers with the chores from a young age. Even as they got older they did not go to pubs and clubs. They did not hang around with boys and as teenagers they did not smoke or drink. They were not supposed to drink alcohol until they were married and I have never seen any girls disobey this rule. For young traveller girls, life was spent at their mother's side, helping with the household chores in preparation for the day when they got married and had a family of their own. It was a completely different story for the lads: they were encouraged to make the most of their freedom and from an early age could come and go as they pleased.

Although most gypsy children went to school, many were withdrawn to keep them away from what was often seen as the damaging influence of the outside world. I knew more than most that school certainly wasn't for everyone – I used to wonder how I would have fared in such an environment. Maybe I would have thrived, putting my talents to practical use, rather than sitting bored in an overheated classroom waiting for the bell to ring, and picked on by teachers who seemed to want us all to be cookie-cutter replicas of the perfect girl or boy.

From birth, traveller girls were taught to have the utmost respect for all their elders and especially for the men of the family. They were taught never to answer back. If a traveller girl was sitting in her trailer watching television and an adult walked in, she would be expected to get up and give up her seat. This respect was not just shown to adult travellers; I've seen gypsy girls offer seats to old people on buses while their non-traveller peers looked on.

It's not an easy life being a gypsy girl and on the one hand they miss out on all the freedoms and opportunities that non-traveller girls take for granted. However, the more I saw, the more I came to see that there were many positives to this way of life. The girls were protected and looked after and did not have to worry about things such as stranger danger, because they didn't roam the streets and get in trouble like I did when I was younger. I often wonder what would have happened to me if I had grown up living with the same kind of rules gypsy girls lived by. I know I wouldn't have been attacked and I would probably have done better at school. Life would have been very different. But also fate would then not have brought me into contact with Pat.

And by that point, a few weeks after the christening, we were becoming more understanding of each other and more secure. We could have a row, one of us would storm off and a day later we would be back together. My feelings for him were becoming deeper. I was falling in love and so was Pat.

We first plucked up the courage to tell each other how we felt after we had been together for around six months.

We were in the cinema (as usual) and had been squabbling over something small. The film was a romantic comedy, *He's Just Not That Into You*, and maybe Pat was caught up in the mood because after he leaned into me and whispered, 'I love you.'

I was still mad at him and I answered, 'Thanks.'

But a couple of weeks later I told him myself. By then I knew that Pat would in one way or another be a big part of my life and I couldn't imagine living without him.

# 13

## Learning the Ropes

By the summer of 2009 not a day went by when Pat and I were not together at some point. We had some hilarious dates. One day he surprised me by driving us to Knowsley Safari Park near Liverpool. We went in the van, which was a bit beaten up and rusty, and as we drove into the monkey enclosure a troop of apes descended on us and started to pick away at loose bits of bodywork. Pat tried to bang on the windows to scare them off but they just hooted at him and ran off with one of the windscreen wipers.

On his nineteenth birthday that year I vowed to make it special for him and invited him round for a birthday surprise.

'Don't be late,' I teased. 'I've made a special effort.'

Pat's eyes lit up and he said he'd be there on the dot of 5 p.m.

We shouldn't have really been alone together, but Mum

had only gone out for a little while so I set about decorating the front room with streamers, banners and balloons.

The surprise was a chocolate fountain I had bought from Argos. I carefully read the instructions and set it up on the table in the middle of the room along with a birthday cake. It was all ready for when Pat arrived, with a waterfall of yummy liquid chocolate cascading from it. I cut up chunks of fruit and placed them carefully on plates along with marshmallows to dip in the melted chocolate. As it warmed up the smell in the house was mouth-watering and, for added romantic effect, I placed candles around the room.

When Pat sent a text just before five o'clock to tell me he was on his way, I lit the candles on the cake and waited excitedly to see his face when he walked through the door. What I didn't realise was that, although he was nearby, he had stopped to talk to a friend and by the time he arrived half an hour later, all the candles had burnt down and his cake was covered in pools of wax. I was in a mood with him and half-jokingly stamped my foot on the floor when he giggled at the sad sight of the cake. The sharp motion made the table shake and we watched horror-struck as the chocolate fountain jumped in the air and tipped over on its side. Melted chocolate splattered over Mum's cream rug and sprayed up the walls and on to the ceiling.

'Oh no,' I gasped as I tried to right the machine and got covered in hot chocolate myself.

Once I had managed to turn it off I bent down to start mopping up the chocolate in a vain effort to stop it staining and as I did, my hair fell into one of the only remaining lit candles and started to sizzle. Pat ran over and began to beat out the flames. It would have been hilarious if it hadn't happened to me and although Pat was laughing after the disaster of my burning hair had been averted, I failed to see the funny side. I thought Mum would be furious but she saw the funny side of it too and when she came home as we started to clean up she laughed and told us to leave it until the gloop had solidified. I spent the next morning picking lumps of chocolate from the rug and carpet.

Despite our misunderstandings, I was deeply in love with my man. He was 19 and I was 16 and I didn't realise just how much I depended on him until he had to return to Scotland for a few weeks in the summer to help an uncle with some work.

I still went to the site most days to see Karen and Chantelle but my heart ached for Pat. The place was empty without him. Since we had started courting we hadn't been apart and I was shocked at how much I missed him. It was during those days that I realised I wanted Pat to be a permanent part of my life and although we had not spoken about marriage, I really couldn't see how I could ever not be with him. I wanted to show him how I felt and I wanted to prove to him that I was serious about him.

I made the decision to have a tattoo with his name on it. I could think of no better way to show him that I wanted to be with him permanently.

Pat and I had spoken about tattoos before and he told me that he didn't like them. Traveller girls are forbidden by their parents to have them. You don't see many girls with them and even fake ones were frowned upon. Chantelle had a fake one once and her father told her to wash it off – and that was when she was an adult with her own child. So I knew that not everyone in my second family would approve of what I was going to do.

Travellers believe that tattoos ruin women's bodies. I had always found that an odd way of thinking because so many traveller men have homemade tattoos that look worse than anything you would have inked in a professional tattoo parlour.

But I was adamant. Although I was with Pat and I was his girl, and when I was with him I tried to adhere to traveller rules, I was and always will be a non-traveller and in my culture and background, tattoos were acceptable so, while Pat was away, I went to a local tattoo parlour and had *Patrick* written across the back of my neck. I had to lie about my age and as the painful needle scratched the soft flesh of my neck I consoled myself with the thought that I was making a statement about the man I loved.

When Pat came back from Scotland I was relieved. It had seemed like he had been away for an eternity and I didn't think I could bear to be parted from him again. He came to my house as soon as he arrived back and we held each other for an age. I had missed his smile, his laugh, his arms, his scent. I had missed every atom of him and it was wonderful to be back in his arms again where I knew I belonged.

As we chatted about what we had both been up to I started to scratch the back of my neck hoping Pat would look, but he was too caught up telling me stories about his travels across the border.

'My hair's itching, babe,' I said to him. 'Can you flick it up, please?'

He looked at me as if I was mad.

I had to think on the spot. 'Can you do it, cos I've... er... hurt my shoulder and it's painful when I raise my arm.'

Pat reached around behind me and brushed my long hair away from the back of my neck.

He was silent for a moment.

'Is that real?' he asked eventually.

'Yes,' I answered. 'I wanted you to know how much you mean to me.'

'Thank you,' he said softly.

He understood the sentiment behind my decision to have the tattoo and he was grateful. His kissed my neck gently.

In fact, Pat respected all my decisions whatever I chose to do and would never try and stand in the way of my independence. He would discuss something with me and try and convince me against certain things if he disagreed, but he would never forbid me doing something I wanted to do and so he accepted the tattoo in the way it was meant, as a sign of my commitment to him. At 16, I felt I had a reached a point in my life where I could make decisions about my future and the tattoo was perhaps the first big statement I made to the world about how I felt about Pat.

Although I was old enough to be intimate with Pat, I respected myself too much to give myself to him and had always believed that intimacy should come with marriage. It's a belief I share with all traveller girls, and any who do have sexual relations before they marry are seen as dirty. They are expected to save themselves for marriage. That is why Pat and me were not allowed to spend time alone together on the site. Even though we were going steady, I was still not allowed to go into his trailer. In the traveller world, contact between men and women is carried out under strict conditions.

If, for example, a traveller woman was alone in a trailer with a man who was not her husband for whatever reason, she would be expected to keep the blinds up or curtains open, just so others could make sure she was not misbehaving.

Learning these rules felt like going back to school at times.

I discovered that traveller girls were not taught about reproduction and sexual health until very late in life. I was shocked to discover that some teenagers still believed they were found by their parents in pea pods or strawberry fields because that's what they had been taught all their lives.

Some parents would take their children out of school over the period where they would be taught sex education in the hope that they didn't learn about it. Parents went out of their way to ensure their children retained their innocence. Any talk that might relate vaguely to sex or reproduction was kept amongst the womenfolk. A woman or girl would never mention anything to do with her body in front of a man. Even talk about having a baby had to go through specific channels, usually through the matriarch of the family to the head of the household, so if, for example, a gypsy girl was carrying a child, she wouldn't tell her father, she would tell her mother who would then tell her father. In fact, even the 'P' word itself is considered offensive – traveller women instead use the word 'expecting'.

Despite the amazing and sometimes revealing clothes gypsy women wore, when it came to maternity wear, the bump was expected to be covered. Displaying it was frowned upon, even to the extent of posing for family pictures holding the bump.

One rule that I had trouble remembering related to watching television or films when men were present. If the content referred to anything sexual, no matter how obscure, women were expected to leave the room or change the channel. So if, for instance, a woman traveller was in a trailer and Jeremy Kyle was on the television talking about DNA tests and a man walked in, she would be expected to change the channel. The same would apply if an advert for sanitary towels came on.

Some travellers even interpreted the rule if, say, there was a couple kissing on *Corrie* and the inference was that the kissing would lead to something else. It was very old-fashioned and sometimes confusing and I discovered that the rule even extended to animated characters.

Pat and I had joined a mixed group of travellers for a trip to see *Ice Age 3* and we were all sitting together in the cinema having fun. I had been whispering to Pat and laughing at him in his 3-D glasses and not paying too much attention to the film when I felt a nudge in my arm. It was Chantelle, who was sitting on the other side of me.

'Come on,' she whispered.

I didn't understand what she meant but looked over her shoulder and saw the girls from the group all get up and shuffle along the row as if they were leaving.

'What's the matter?' I asked her, confused.

She seemed anxious and embarrassed. 'We need to go to the loo,' she indicated, nodding her head to the exit.

Then I looked at the screen and realised what was happening. Hopefully I won't spoil it for anyone who hasn't seen it but in the movie a female elephant has a baby. It is a kids' film, and obviously you do not see the baby elephant coming out, but because the subject was childbirth and because there were traveller men present, the girls needed to leave.

I looked at Pat and shrugged, apologised to the other people in the row who must have wondered what was going on, and joined Chantelle outside until we could be sure the scene was over, at which point we re-entered the cinema.

It was a slightly surreal experience but explains why so many traveller girls grow up with a fixation with Disney films and theatrical weddings. Even in their teenage years and into their twenties that is often the only kind of romance they have ever experienced.

By that stage of our relationship I was on a steep learning curve and Pat's lovely nan realised how serious we both were about each other and bought me a book about traveller life to help me learn the ropes. It had a helpful glossary at the back, which I still refer to today to help me understand some of the traveller words I hear.

Travellers have a whole language of their own and I learnt that *bal* is hair, *chave* is a child, to *gell* is to go, *kushtie* is good and *mullered* means dead. Pat started teaching me phrases and we would laugh together as I messed up the pronunciation.

My education in the language and customs didn't always go as smoothly as I would have wished but Pat was always patient and encouraging. The problem was that apart from the book Pat's nan gave me, there is no simple guide to traveller life and no one sits you down and tells you everything, so often I had to learn through trial and error.

One of my biggest faux pas happened because no one explained about traveller swearing customs. Travellers have words that they find hugely offensive just like non-travellers. While we may shudder at the C-word, the worse insult you could direct at a traveller man is any word that refers to the male 'bits'. Mention any word like that in the company of travellers and you will not be welcome.

I didn't know any of this before I met Pat. I was brought up with those kinds of words; my brothers used them all the time and they were a fairly common part of my vocabulary.

I came to understand just how offensive those words are during an animated conversation with Pat's family one day. We were discussing someone, an acquaintance that we all knew. He must have been unpopular because we were all bitching about him.

'Yeah,' I agreed, adding my opinion, 'he's a d**khead.'

The room suddenly went very quiet and there were audible gasps. I had no idea what had just happened but it was obvious from the reaction that I had said something I wasn't supposed to.

Karen indicated to Pat that perhaps he should explain and he gently led me outside the trailer and gave me a lesson in gypsy etiquette.

'You can't say that, especially in front of men,' he said gently.

'Say what?' I asked, genuinely confused.

'What you just said, that name you just called the man. You can't refer to *that* part of the body. It's really offensive, it makes you look bad.'

I nodded and I learnt my lesson, but it puzzled me because it was acceptable to use words that refer to a woman's private parts. It seemed a bit unfair.

In the end there was no harm done. Pat's family understood and knew that I didn't mean to offend them and when I walked back in the trailer Karen winked at me and we carried on as if nothing had happened.

Despite hiccups like that I was learning fast and Pat and I were falling deeper and deeper in love. I had by then stopped working in Greggs. I didn't see eye to eye with one of the other staff members there and in the end decided to hand in my notice rather than be miserable every day. Instead I started working in one of the local pubs. Even though I was only 16 I looked a lot older and no one bothered to check my ID.

It was a part-time job and I worked the late afternoon and early evening shift. Most of the nights I was behind the bar Pat would come in and say hello, perch himself at the end of the bar and have a pint. He was a great one for talking to the regulars and the old men who made the pub their second home.

Although the pub I worked in welcomed him and didn't mind serving travellers, there were other pubs in town where travellers were barred. In any town near any site travellers have to learn where they are welcome and where to steer clear of. One night we went to a bar in town and the bouncers said I could go in but Pat couldn't. I asked why and they didn't hide their prejudice.

'No gypsies allowed,' they growled.

I pointed out to them the stupidity of allowing someone in who is underage but barring someone else who is legally allowed to drink.

I soon discovered that it wasn't always the travellers who kept the outside world at arm's length, it was the rest of my community shunning the travellers.

Pat was trusted and most of the businesses around the town knew him; even the local kebab shop trusted him enough to allow him to run up a tab, which he paid off once a month. But outside of the town it was a different story.

I learned just how suspicious people could be soon after we started dating and went to a supermarket. Normally we used the Tesco near the site and the staff there knew Pat, but this was in a different town and as we walked down the aisle I started to get the uncomfortable feeling that we were being watched.

I looked around to see if there was anyone following us and as I did I noticed a flash of blue from the corner of the aisle. As we walked further I turned again, quicker this time, and saw the security guard in a blue uniform quickly pretend to look in the opposite direction. It was almost comical.

We carried on doing our shopping and every so often I'd look around and the guard would either be standing several feet behind us looking away or I would just catch him disappear around a corner or behind a display.

'He's following us,' I pointed out to Pat.

'I know, they always do,' he shrugged.

After that I kept an eye out in different shops and began to notice that Pat was right. It wasn't always guards in uniform; sometimes it was undercover store detectives, but each time it was the same. We'd be shadowed through the shop until we made our purchases and left.

It used to annoy me but now I just laugh about it; me and Pat, public enemies numbers one and two!

# 14

## A Proposal

How do you know when you are in love if you have never
loved anyone before? How do you describe love?

I was just 16 and although as far as boys and romance
were concerned I was naive and totally inexperienced, I
knew I was in love with Pat. He was my first and only
love and my feelings for him grew from those early giddy
days of infatuation into deeper feelings which I had never
felt before.

I'm not one to analyse my emotions and work out
what makes me feel a certain way so it's hard for someone
like me to explain what love means to me. But I felt happy
when I was with Pat, and sad when I wasn't. When we
were apart, I pined and I needed to be with him and when
we were together, I was a better person, a happier and
more fulfilled person. Being with him felt natural, as if it
was meant to be.

I believe in love at first sight and I believe that there is someone for everyone, that each one of us has a perfect partner out there waiting to be discovered. Most of us never find that magical person and instead settle for second best. But I was one of the lucky ones: I had found my Mr Right and I knew as the summer of 2009 began to turn to autumn that Pat and I were soulmates.

I hoped Pat felt the same. I had a strong feeling that he did but I sometimes wondered whether the fact that I was a non-traveller would mean we could not be together for ever. Deep down I thought that maybe the gap between our two lifestyles and cultures would be too wide to bridge.

However, it was obvious we were both committed to each other and, as in most committed relationships, talk sometimes turned to marriage and weddings. There was no one big conversation where the subject was broached; it just slowly became part of the vocabulary of our relationship. We would be discussing a friend's wedding and then conversation would steer towards our own plans.

'If we ever got married, what type of wedding do you reckon we would have?' I'd ask.

Pat never shirked away from the subject, he was more than eager to talk about it, and as the months went on it just became a natural thing to discuss.

Despite my fears that the differences in our cultures would ultimately push us apart, I knew that Pat would never have introduced me to his family and made me part of his traveller life if he was not 100 per cent committed and serious about our future together. That is the traveller way.

Just by inviting me to be part of his life was a huge show of commitment from him. In a traveller relationship, you know where you stand. There is no sitting at home waiting for the phone to ring and wondering if your fella is serious or not. It is all or nothing with traveller boys – you are either in or out. And if you were in, that meant that you were seen as marriage material.

That was also why travellers tended to marry young. As a rule they did not play the field, their way was to find a partner and settle down and raise a family. Travellers didn't go to uni, go on gap years and then spend years working at a career. The men usually went into the family business, as scrap merchants or landscape gardeners or builders, and the women left school early and stayed at home. In fact it was rare to see an unmarried traveller girl in her mid-twenties, by then they were usually married off and the later they left it, the harder it was for them to find a husband because practically all of the boys had married young as well.

I yearned for Pat when I didn't see him. In the evenings when we said our goodbyes I felt lost and alone, not because of any physical desire, but because I just felt that my natural place was with him.

We wanted to spend all our time together and when we were apart we counted the hours until we were together again.

In a traveller relationship you did not have the luxury of living with someone first to find out if you are compatible before you married them. You could not spend nights together, you could not go away on romantic holidays. You found out whether you were with the right person in bite-sized chunks and by instinct. At the end of every evening you said goodbye until the next day. I went home to Mum or Dad, and Pat went to his trailer with John Thomas and Levi.

Pat found sharing with his younger brothers both amusing and annoying in equal measure. As a woman I was not allowed in their trailer (the rule even applied later when we got engaged). So I could only imagine what it was like but I sometimes got the impression it was like an episode of *Men Behaving Badly*.

One day Pat came to pick me up in the morning after a night in the trailer and I noticed he had no eyebrows. It looked awful and I gasped when I saw him.

'What have you done to yourself, Pat? You look like a weirdo,' I frowned.

He looked sheepish and shrugged. 'It wasn't me, the boys shaved them off while I was asleep,' he explained. Then he told me that it was not just him missing eyebrows that morning. Both John Thomas and Levi had been subjected to matching makeovers.

He recounted the story. He'd been in a deep sleep but in the early hours of the morning had woken because his eye was stinging and felt like it had soap in it. As he reached up to scratch, his brow felt strange and when he ran his fingertips across it he realised one of his eyebrows was missing.

'I just assumed it was John Thomas, it's the kind of thing he'd do,' Pat explained.

Livid, he'd gone into John Thomas's room. He was lying in bed asleep. Pat found a razor, pinned his snoozing brother down and before John Thomas could wake up and realise what was happening to him he had shaved both his eyebrows off.

Disorientated and half asleep John Thomas sat up and the boys started arguing until Pat became convinced that his brother's protests of innocence were actually genuine.

'I'm telling you I didn't do it,' John Thomas implored. 'I've been asleep.'

Both standing there in the gloom, one with a single eyebrow and the other with none, the brothers realised who the real culprit was: their little brother Levi. They both stormed into his room and found him hiding under the sheets of his bunk. He'd been listening to their row and realised it was only a matter of time before they worked out who the guilty party really was.

Pat and John Thomas then took it in turns to shave off one of Levi's eyebrows. And in the morning, when Pat woke and looked at himself in the mirror, he thought it looked odd to just have one eyebrow so he shaved his remaining one off to even up the look.

I tutted, but couldn't help giggling. They were like a bunch of unruly children and without any adults in the trailer to tell them off, they got away with acting like that. Their relationship made me think about my brothers and how we used to play tricks on each other. I felt a pang when I thought of the years we had been separated – perhaps everything would have been better if Dad had gone away and lived in one trailer, Mum had moved into another, and we kids moved into a third!

Pat didn't share my sentimentality, however, and would often moan about the practical jokes and the mess. The boys didn't clean or cook for themselves. Their mum did that and Pat usually ate with me. At 16, if I wasn't working in the pub, I would prepare his tea for when he came home from work and we would eat together before he went back to the trailer site. I had been used to cooking for myself and my brothers if Mum was working, so it seemed natural to cook for Pat as well. We were like an old married couple even then!

For us it all seemed very normal, but the reality was that there was something very different about our relationship. While other couples our age could sneak nights together, we were separated during the hours of darkness by Pat's culture. The type of intimacy my non-traveller friends were able to experiment with was forbidden for us. As far as I was concerned this was never a problem. We both respected ourselves and each other too much to give away our innocence cheaply. According to traveller rules, if we wanted to go away together we would have to go chaperoned by parents and be separated at night.

Dad understood this when he invited me and Pat to a camping holiday in North Wales with him and my brothers.

The plan was for us to meet them at the campsite with our tent and equipment and spend the weekend with them. It would be our first proper weekend away and at night I would stay in my tent with Dad while Pat bunked down with Dean and Brian.

Excitedly we packed our gear and set out early in the morning for the three-hour drive to the campsite. On the way we planned romantic walks on the beach, barbecues and trips to the amusement arcades.

'It'll be our first proper holiday,' I smiled.

By then Pat had become as much a part of my family as I was of his. My brothers enjoyed his company and he had my dad's approval. Any early reservations that they had about him had gone. My dad could see that Pat adored me and was intent on looking after me and he knew that we were both very serious about each other. The age gap might have concerned both him and my mum to begin with but they could see his intentions towards me were honourable.

When we arrived at the campsite we left our camping gear in the van and headed straight to the beach to meet everyone. The sun was shining and before long we were larking around like kids, splashing about in the waves and having fun.

As I paddled out into the freezing water, Dad decided it would be a fun trick to creep up behind me with a bucket of water and drench me.

I squealed as I got a soaking and Pat stood on the beach with my brothers laughing at my misfortune.

'Thanks a lot!' I yelled. 'You're supposed to be protecting me!'

Pat shrugged. He wasn't about to step in and take sides against my dad. Gypsies respected family bonds too much to get involved in tussles between members of other people's families.

Later that afternoon, we headed back to the campsite where Pat pitched the tent next to my dad's. I was dry by then and we started to discuss our sleeping arrangements.

'You might as well put your sleeping bag in my tent,' said Dad.

'Where's the sleeping bag, Pat?' I called.

Pat looked perplexed. 'You packed it,' he answered.

I knew I hadn't. 'No you did,' I answered.

We looked at each other. We'd forgotten the sleeping bags.

Dad laughed. 'What are you going to sleep in? A T-shirt and shorts?' he said.

It was North Wales in late summer, not the tropics. Even though the sun was out neither of us fancied a night with no proper sleeping cover and so we set off to the local shops to try and find somewhere that sold sleeping bags.

Two hours later we were defeated. We had tried everywhere and returned to the campsite dejected. We realised we couldn't stay and our long weekend together had turned into a badly organised day trip. We drove back as the sun was setting. There was one thought that made the journey home bearable. I had always prided myself on my appearance and tried to look my best for Pat whenever we were together. I loved my make-up and I loved my clothes and at least Pat wouldn't have to see me first thing in the morning after a night roughing it in a tent.

A few days later he made up for the disappointment by pitching the tent in my mum's lounge and we spent an afternoon like two children, camping in the front room and watching telly in the tent. It was like I was making up for that summer I had lost when I was attacked. It was fun, if not a little silly, and for that short period of time we could forget about the world around us. I felt that my childhood had ended so abruptly, and now I was experiencing life like a little kid again; everything seemed full of wonder and promise. Camping in our living room made me remember that time when I was 11 and Pat brought around a whole lot of Kinder chocolate and we stuffed them into our faces. Pat had helped me forget about my cares then, and he was helping me dig up that part of myself that had been buried under my troubles.

We seemed to bring out the best in each other when we were together. I rediscovered my sense of fun when I was with Pat and he in turn was like a big kid sometimes and would do all he could to make me laugh.

As the months went by and the year came to a close we both thought more and more about the future. If we wanted to be together as a proper couple we would need to marry.

I would be lying if I said I didn't have some reservations. I would never expect Pat to abandon his way of life, he was a traveller and he'll always be a traveller. I would have to make sacrifices for him that most other brides never had to. I would have to totally change my way of life and live in a trailer with him, on a site with his family. For a 16-year-old girl, it would be a huge change of lifestyle.

I had never spent a night on the site and although I was there almost every day, I realised that was very different from living there full time. I was not a gypsy, I would never be a gypsy; you are born a gypsy, you do not become one. And I didn't want to be something I was not. I have never professed to be a gypsy and I sometimes worried whether the fact that I could never be the type of girl that his family expected Pat to be with since the day he was born would eventually tear us apart.

And yet I had found a peace and belonging in the gypsy community that I had never experienced anywhere else in my life. The rules sometimes seemed severe. I knew living in a trailer was not the easiest way of life. But as far as I could see the benefits far outweighed the disadvantages. I knew that I would probably encounter some prejudice, both from travellers and non-travellers. Money would be tight and winters would be hard but in exchange I would have the support of a new, loving family and most importantly I would have a future with the man I loved. And he was committed to looking after me.

As 2009 ended, our dedication to each other was not in doubt. We planned to celebrate New Year's Eve at a travellers' do in a pub in St Helens. Pat's family would be there and it would be a traditional party.

Before we went we had a meal together in a local restaurant and Pat seemed strange.

He steered the conversation to marriage and children.

'What would be your ideal wedding?' he asked.

I was never one of those children who obsessed about weddings when I was younger but like all girls I had thought about the subject in the past and more so since I met Pat. I didn't watch Disney movies and wasn't fixated with princess brides but I did know that if and when I did get married I would want to do it in a big, stunning dress.

I had loved Katie Price's wedding to Peter Andre and thought that her dress and her glass carriage were classy and stylish and made the right statement.

'You only get married once,' I explained to Pat. 'Why do it in a normal dress? You can wear normal dresses all the time. Your wedding day should be special. It should be a day you will never forget.'

Pat nodded. He seemed pleased with my answer.

Later, after the meal, we walked to the party. It was a chilly night, and with my short fitted tight dress and heels I was underdressed and cold.

'Can I have your jacket please, babe?' I asked.

Normally Pat would have wrapped me in it to keep me warm. But he looked stricken when I asked. 'Let's walk a bit faster, that will warm you up,' he said, and started to walk ahead.

He continued acting strangely when we arrived. He refused to take off his jacket and, in the steamy pub, became hotter and more anxious as the hours passed.

I pulled Karen to one side. 'Pat's acting really strange,' I said. 'Is he okay?'

'I think so,' his mum replied. 'Maybe he's got something important on his mind.' She winked and smiled, leaving me even more perplexed.

After a few Cheeky Vimtos I was getting in the party mood. I grabbed Pat for a dance.

'What's wrong with you tonight?' I asked him. 'You seem like you don't want to be here, would you rather we leave?'

'Of course not,' he said. 'This is the most important night of the year.'

I didn't understand what he was talking about. All the cryptic messages were beginning to confuse me, but I found out the reason for his strange behaviour two hours later as the clock ticked down to midnight.

The room became a huddle of people, crowded on the dance floor as the last seconds of 2009 ticked away.

'Five... four... three... two... one...' we chanted together. And as the peals of Big Ben striking midnight rung out over the PA system I turned to give my man a New Year's kiss. Except he wasn't there. Then I looked down. Pat was on one knee in front of me, looking up into my face; the emotion sparkling in his eyes matched the sparkle of the diamond set in the ring he was holding in his hand and offering towards me.

Above the roar of cheers and the crack of party poppers he shouted, 'Sam Norton, you know I love you and I want to spend the rest of my life with you. Will you do me the honour of becoming my wife?'

All around people were shouting, kissing and dancing. I was in a bubble. I didn't hear any of it. My focus in those seconds was on Pat, his eyes and his words. I felt my heart expand in my chest. It filled with love and in the first seconds of 2010 I saw my future.

'Yes,' I wept. 'I will.'

# 15

## Making Plans

As everyone around us joined hands and started singing
'Auld Lang Syne', Pat stood and held me. We kissed
tenderly and hugged so tightly I felt as if we were fused
into one body. I didn't want to let him go.

Tears were streaming down my face.

'That's why you didn't want to take your jacket off,'
I sniffed.

Bless him, he had been scared he'd lose the ring.
The ring! I hadn't even looked at it properly. He lifted
the dainty jewellery box towards me so I could get a
better peek.

I gasped. It was stunning. The single diamond twinkled under the disco lights.

'Oh my God, Pat, it must have cost a fortune. It's
beautiful.' I was sobbing with joy.

Pat shrugged. 'You are priceless, Princess, you only
deserve the best,' he smiled.

Then I had a thought. 'My dad,' I worried. 'Have you asked my dad?'

When it came to wedding etiquette I had strong views about doing things the correct way and I always believed that I would only ever marry a man who came with my dad's seal of approval because, after all, Dad would be the one to walk me down the aisle. I knew Dad liked and approved of Pat but I had never told him I wanted to settle down with him. What if Dad didn't want me to marry a traveller? What if Dad thought I was too young to get married?

'It's okay,' reassured Pat. 'I asked him. I went round and spoke to him and told him that I wanted to marry you and asked for his blessing. He was happy for both of us.'

They were the words I longed to hear.

Meanwhile, word spread around the room. Pat's mum, dad, sister, brothers, nan, aunts, uncles and cousins all came over throughout the rest of the night to offer congratulations and to buy us drinks. It was a riotous night. The goodwill was staggering. It seemed everyone wanted to shake Pat's hand and give me a hug. I realised then just how big my new family was going to be. There were people there introducing themselves as relatives that I had never seen before; Pat didn't know some of them either but in traveller tradition, they were all family. And because they were family they were all happy for us. There were no guarded looks or negative comments about a traveller marrying a non-traveller.

The rest of the night passed in a blur.

I stayed at my dad's house that night and rolled home in the early hours of the morning with my head swimming. I was exhausted, but I couldn't sleep a wink. My mind was spinning.

I reached for my phone and typed out a text message to Pat.

*You've made me the happiest girl in the world. I'll love you till I die.*

A few seconds later I got a reply.

*Happy New Year, wife-to-be*, it read.

The following morning as I was getting ready I heard a knock on the door followed by Pat's familiar voice as he wished my dad Happy New Year. I raced downstairs and gave my brand-new fiancé a hug.

'Dad,' I said, 'we've got something we need to tell you.'

Dad smiled; he knew what I was going to say but he let me speak. I wanted to be the one to tell him.

'Pat proposed last night. We're getting married.'

Dad smiled and hugged me. Then he shook Pat's hand.

'Look after her,' he said. 'She's a precious girl.'

Pat nodded. 'I know,' he said. 'I will be the best husband ever.'

Dad put his arms around us both.

'So,' he asked, 'when's the wedding?'

Pat and I looked at each other. We had only been engaged for a few hours and hadn't yet got round to thinking about the details. We didn't know. We laughed.

'I guess we have some planning to do,' I giggled.

Later that day Pat drove me to Mum's. She didn't know what had happened the night before and it was time to tell her. For some reason I felt much more nervous about telling Mum than I did about telling Dad or any of Pat's family. Maybe it was because Mum had never been married. It wasn't that she was anti-marriage, she just never found the right man. I worried what her reaction would be. I was still only 16, and my eighteenth birthday was 15 months away; it would be natural for her to think that I was far too young to settle down. And although she had never shown any prejudice towards Pat's traveller roots, I worried that when it came to the crunch, she would be unhappy about me marrying into what was an alien way of life for most non-travellers. The only time I'd spent living in caravans before I met Pat was in chalets and mobile homes on holiday parks. Living in a trailer permanently was an entirely different proposition.

By the time we arrived at Mum's front door I was a bag of nerves.

'You tell her,' I ordered Pat.

'What's wrong?' he replied. 'Are you ashamed of me?'

'Of course I'm not,' I said. 'I just feel too nervous. It'll sound better coming from you.'

We went in and sat down in the lounge with a cup of tea.

'How was your night?' Mum asked.

'It was lovely thanks... Pat's got something to tell you,' I blurted.

Pat shifted nervously on the sofa.

'Linda,' he said, 'last night I asked Sam to marry me. And she said yes. We're both really happy and I hope you will be too.'

Mum looked at us both. I couldn't read her face. What was she thinking? Then a smile spread across her lips.

'Congratulations,' she squealed, 'that's wonderful news.'

I felt myself breathe a sigh of relief. With Mum and Dad's approval given, I knew then it was time to start planning.

Later that week we sat down and began to think seriously about what we wanted for our wedding day and when to do it.

I was still working in the pub and Pat was busy with his business but neither of us was making the kind of money that would allow us to have the wedding of our dreams any time soon.

'We need plenty of time to save,' I told Pat. 'I don't want a short registry office wedding. I want a church wedding and I want it to be a special day.'

Pat agreed: if it meant we would have to wait then so be it. We were in no rush and although it meant we could not live together as soon as we wanted to, we planned out a budget and realised it would take over a year to save enough for the type of day we both wanted. The date was set for Valentine's Day 2011. We had just over a year.

We both realised what the implications would be. Even though we were engaged to be married, it still would not alter the fact that it would be 13 months before we could spend a night together. And there was no question of trying to sneak a night together before the wedding. I didn't want to be seen as dirty on my wedding day. I'd even heard the story of a girl who travelled in a car to Scotland overnight with her boyfriend and as a result had her honour called into question – even though all that had happened was that she slept while he drove.

'I'd wait for ever for you, Princess,' Pat assured me.

By this point Pat knew all there was to know about me. I had told him about the attack. We had taken a drive to a place called Billinge Hill, a local beauty spot that looked out over the town. From the vantage point at the top of the hill you could see the town spread out below and as we sat there with the streetlights twinkling below us like a blanket of orange stars I explained what had happened.

'I don't want us to have any secrets,' I told him after recounting the painful details.

'I respect you, whatever has happened in the past. It changes nothing,' Pat told me.

They were the words I needed to hear.

A few days after we set the initial date and I had time to think, I realised something. If we were going to get married in February, it would mean that we would not be together over Christmas. I would still be at Mum's and Pat would still be living in the trailer with his brothers. And the time when I found it hardest of all being away from Pat was over Christmas. I longed for the day when I could wake up on Christmas morning with my husband, when we could open our presents together in our own home, rather than shuttle between parents.

We discussed it and Pat felt the same, so we agreed we would move the date and get married on 4 December

2010. Were we crazy? I would still only be 17 – very young in non-traveller society to get married.

Even with such a seemingly long time to plan there were certain things we had to book sooner rather than later.

After seeing Katie Price's wedding I had set my heart on being taken to church in a pink fairy-tale horse-drawn carriage. And after a few enquiries I found one in the area that during the summer months was booked up two years in advance but available on the date we had set.

'I'll take it,' I said quickly.

I put the phone down and squealed with excitement. That was it, the first part of the wedding jigsaw was in place. It suddenly seemed real.

A few months after the proposal Pat came round to my house one evening with a newspaper and showed me the TV listings.

'We have to watch this,' he said, pointing out a show called *My Big Fat Gypsy Wedding*. It was a documentary on Channel 4, which promised to go behind the scenes and show what happens at traveller weddings.

I'd seen photos and videos of some lavish traveller weddings but as far as I knew, non-travellers had big lavish weddings too. Some travellers had small weddings. The only thing that struck me as any different about traveller weddings was the way the girls dressed. They always seemed to make much more of an effort than settled people.

So that night we sat down and watched the show. It was enjoyable, a bit snooty, but on balance it was a fair portrayal of traveller life.

The next day the papers were full of stories about the show: people were in shock about some of the lengths the girls went to, to stand out on their wedding day, and also about some of the clothes the younger girls were wearing. Commentators criticised them for being too young to wear revealing clothes. I couldn't see what the fuss was about. The girls were dressing up because they wanted to look good and because they were not usually allowed out to meet boys. But at the core of every traveller girl is the idea of honour and of being innocent, so where was the harm?

A short time after the programme was broadcast, I had my own opportunity to experience a gypsy wedding for myself. One of the girls who lived on the site, Agnes, was getting married and Pat and I were invited. She was 18 and had lived with her parents all her life. After the wedding day she would move to a new trailer with her husband in St Helens. I was excited about the prospect of going because it would give me some ideas for my own wedding day.

As I had already learned, the first dilemma of any gypsy function is what to wear.

Pat immediately sensed my anxiety. 'We'd better go shopping,' he said.

But it wasn't a trip to Cheater Mill. The designer gear there was for every day; for weddings and functions I needed something that would stand out more than a fake Dior dress.

Many of the local traveller girls shopped in a posh frock shop in nearby Ashford. The boutique sold the kind of clothes you do not see on the high street. They are bold and ultra-fashionable, more like costumes from music videos or movies. The shop does a roaring trade supplying the tastes of the local traveller community and I was beginning to learn that along with clothes shops, there was a whole network of stores that travellers preferred to use. They would buy furniture, trailers and vehicles from specific suppliers. It was almost like an approved list. Many shops were kept in business by the traveller community.

We went along to the clothes shop on a Saturday afternoon and it was full. You could spot the traveller girls picking out their dresses. They would think nothing of spending hundreds on an outfit that they would probably only wear once. I chose a striking skintight gold sequinned mini-dress for the occasion.

On the wedding day Agnes looked amazing. She got ready in a hotel and wore an incredible white dress with a long flowing train. She arrived in church in a horse-drawn carriage and the guests cheered after the vicar pronounced them man and wife.

The reception was in a local social club and was a riot of colour and exotic outfits. I started to realise why some traveller brides insist on such big dresses. Perhaps it was the only way they could guarantee to not be upstaged by the guests!

At the wedding, in true traveller fashion, the men and women sat apart. Later in the evening, however, the boys and girls started to mix. I wondered if this wedding would lead to others. I had heard about a custom called grabbing, where traveller boys were supposed to force girls into kissing them. It was part of the courtship ritual, almost like play-acting. It did happen but it wasn't common and I didn't see any of it at the wedding. Pat explained that although he didn't agree with it, it was just a thing that some teenagers would do. A girl would chat to a boy, they would figure out that they liked each other, and then she would make a point of walking off on her own. The boy would follow, get her on her own and try and kiss her. It was for show and he explained that a girl wouldn't get grabbed if she didn't want to be grabbed.

As the band played the last slow songs I grabbed Pat myself and we danced together.

I looked over at the newlyweds.

'That'll be us soon,' I said, nuzzling into his neck.

I knew it was incredibly unusual for a traveller and non-traveller to get married. Even now I do not know any other mixed couples. Some travellers have relationships with non-travellers and even have children together but in my experience they do not marry.

But as far as some of Pat's family were concerned I was already officially a Lee even before we married. Karen now introduced me as her daughter. The first time I heard her say it, my heart skipped a beat. It was as if she were accepting me into her family all over again. And whenever she went shopping and bought something for Chantelle, she would buy something for me as well. She kept an eye out for homeware for us and bought me my first slow cooker. I had never met such a generous person.

I too had started collecting bits for a new home and kept them under my bed at my mum's, neatly packed in boxes.

We were both saving hard and didn't have the money to go out as much as we used to. But Pat still managed to find ways to wow me.

One evening in March he came to pick me up.

'I'm taking you to a show,' he said, smiling.

'What are you talking about?' I asked. Pat wasn't the theatre-going type.

After 20 minutes in the van he put on his lost routine.

'I must have taken a wrong turning somewhere,' he laughed and pulled up in a dark country car park. 'Let's get out and have a look around,' he said.

'Are you mad?' I laughed, but got out the van anyway. I knew he had something up his sleeve. And played along.

He took my hand and led me along a footpath through a wood. Normally I would have been terrified but I trusted Pat with my life and knew he would protect me with his.

At the end of the path there was a wooden bridge over a lake. The water was shimmering as the moonlight reflected off it and lit up the surrounding area. Owls hooted in the darkness.

He led me on to the bridge.

'Look up,' he said gently.

I did and above us was the clearest, most amazing night sky I have ever seen. The moon glowed and the stars were so bright and packed together you could see the clouds of the Milky Way. It didn't look real.

'I wanted to give you the moon and the stars,' he said, holding my hand.

It was at times like that when I had to pinch myself. I couldn't believe how lucky I was. Pat was so romantic and the perfect hubby material. We didn't have to go to fancy restaurants or swanky clubs; we shared everything and talked all the time. We didn't have any secrets.

I knew I was safe in his hands. We had our disagreements and every now and then I still had to keep him on his toes.

Once, a few months after he proposed, I saw a photo of him on Facebook. He was obviously drunk. He was wearing a builder's hat and had his arm around a girl. There was nothing in it but I was livid. He wouldn't expect me to behave like that so why should he be allowed to? He explained that he was just posing for photos and didn't even know the girl but I was seething. He was with me at Mum's house and I threw him out. The following day he turned up with flowers and apologised.

I made a note to check Facebook more often. Which is where I found a message in the spring of 2010 from a television company who were looking for gypsy brides to be in a new series.

The one-off documentary Pat and I had watched had caused such an interest in the traveller world that a TV company had decided to make a series following different travellers as they prepared for their weddings. They also wanted to film christenings and day-to-day life on traveller sites.

They had found my details from the carriage company I had booked and wanted to know if Pat and I would like to be filmed for the documentary.

When he came to Mum's that afternoon I told him.

'They want to follow us around and film our wedding, what do you reckon?'

I was apprehensive but Pat thought it would be fun.

'What's the worst that could happen?' he said. 'We could get famous and at least it will let people see what travellers are really like.'

I was worried that people might think I was trying to be something I am not.

'But I am not a traveller,' I told the producers when we made contact. It didn't matter: they were interested in Pat and me precisely because we came from different cultures. The discussions went on for weeks and finally, in the middle of summer, we agreed.

And then they dropped the bombshell. They needed to film the show before November. If we wanted to be in it we would have to get married in six weeks' time!

# 16

Looking for Inspiration

'So here is my plan.'

Pat and I were at my mum's house in the living room having our tea. After a few sleepless nights worrying about the sudden marriage deadline, I had started to work out in my mind what I wanted our wedding day to be like.

'We'll book St Patrick's in Earlestown as close to November as we can to give us enough time.' I knew I was taking a chance with the weather. The longer we left it, the more chance there was that it would be dull and wet, but we had hardly saved any money so we needed to give ourselves as much time as we could.

Pat nodded.

'I want a theme. I want people to remember our wedding. I want to be a sleeping bride.'

Pat blinked.

'A sleeping bride?' he repeated. I had seen it on *Footballers' Wives* years ago and the scene had always stuck with me.

'Yes. What will happen is this,' I explained. 'I will be lying on a glass bed at the end of the aisle when you come in. I'll be pretending to be asleep. You walk slowly towards me and when you reach me you will bend down and kiss me, I'll open my eyes, pretend to wake and then stand for the vows.'

I loved my plan. It would be an amazing, emotional marriage, I remember sobbing when I watched it on television. And as far as I knew, it had never been replicated in real life. It would be completely unique. People would be talking about it for months. I knew plenty of travellers who had themed their weddings so, I reasoned, why not go the whole hog and have a prop as well? I even toyed with the idea of wearing glass slippers, just to mix up the fairy-tale references – I felt like Cinderella, Sleeping Beauty, Snow White and all the fairy-tale princesses there had ever been, and of course Pat was my Prince Charming.

Pat didn't look convinced.

'I'm not supposed to kiss you until after the vows though, am I?' he said. 'And you can't pretend to be asleep while we are saying them. You need to answer back and be conscious.'

'Well just pretend to kiss me at the beginning to wake me and then we can kiss properly at the end,' I replied.

'Where do we get a glass bed from?' Pat asked.

I hadn't thought through the logistics.

'eBay?' I offered.

To people outside the traveller community my idea would probably sound outrageous. But traveller weddings were about making a statement. They were about showing how important those wedding vows were and the best way to do that was to have a day that people remembered. Outside of the traveller community it's easy to look around and think that marriage has lost some of its seriousness. So many people got divorced and split up. The first hiccup and they were out of there. That's not what travellers believe in and it wasn't what I believed either. Marriage was for life. Once you got hitched you were in it for the long haul. In the traveller community people do not get divorced. Sometimes they separate and move away but they don't get divorced. There is an enormous stigma attached to it.

I knew that my wedding day would be the only wedding day I ever had. So I didn't want to have any half-measures. It was a once-in-a-lifetime deal. There would be no repeats. And that's why I wanted my day to be extra-special, and to reflect Pat's and my personality. The wedding would have been the same whether or not it was being filmed for TV: I wanted a big lavish affair, and I wanted people to come away from my wedding with smiles on their faces. I wanted the world to know how much I love Pat by seeing the effort I had put into our special day and know that I would make the same effort into making our marriage as happy as it could possibly be.

Pat took some convincing about my Sleeping Beauty idea but in the end he came round and for the next week I was glued to the computer, scouring the globe for a glass bed. After several frustrating nights I had to admit to myself that perhaps I had bitten off more than I could chew.

'How's the bed search going?' Pat asked one afternoon.

'I can't find one,' I admitted sulkily. 'I've looked everywhere. You'd think someone somewhere would have one wouldn't you? I can't even find glass slippers.'

It seemed that not everyone shared my idea of what made a romantic wedding day and in the end I had to admit defeat.

Pat sympathised – though I'm sure a small part of him was also very relieved! 'It can still be magical,' he soothed.

Yes, I thought to myself, it can. All I needed was the most amazing dress. And so I started to plan out in my head the biggest and best dress I could imagine.

It needed to be stunning and it needed to have something spectacular about it, an element that made it different from other dresses. I knew what I didn't want. I didn't want something fitted and plain, it had to look like a proper wedding dress, not something you'd wear on a night out. It had to look traditional, but with a modern twist. I didn't yet know exactly what I wanted except that it had to be extraordinary, there had to be something about it that would elevate it above just an ordinary wedding dress. My benchmark was that it would have to make the guests gasp.

I knew that there was an unspoken competition between traveller brides to see who could have the most amazing dress. It got to the point where some of the garments were so heavy and cumbersome the brides could barely move when they wore them. After the walk down the aisle and the first dance they would stay seated for the rest of the day. Other brides proudly wore scars on their hips where the weight of material had gouged into their flesh. They were like torture devices, totally impractical and painful, but, for sheer breathtaking spectacle, you couldn't beat a gypsy dress.

I started out looking on the Internet for inspiration. Disney-themed dresses seemed too plain; they weren't spectacular enough and had been done before. A lot of girls got their inspiration from dresses they had seen in the movies so I googled 'film wedding dresses' and as I flicked through the images one photo immediately caught my eye.

It was from a scene in the Eddie Murphy movie *Coming To America*. I had never seen the film but the dress stopped me in my tracks. I was hypnotised. It was light pink and, although I didn't like the top half, from the waist down it was amazing. It must have been 10 feet in diameter and the skirt was swathed in cascades of exotic cloth. The veil swept over the top of the bride's head and flowed down her back. It looked like a wave of material, a tsunami of satin and taffeta. I had found my perfect style and printed out an image to show Pat's mum.

'Oh Sam, it's gorgeous,' she said. 'It will look stunning.'

But still I thought the design needed something, a few more extra tweaks to make it stand out even more. Something to light it up. And that was when I had my Eureka moment – lights!

I would have an illuminated dress. It made perfect sense. It would be a winter wedding and so twinkling lights would give the dress a frosty, Christmassy feel. I would keep it a secret until later in the evening when it got dark and then I would surprise everyone by lighting myself up.

But that wasn't enough. I had also heard of some traveller weddings where the brides had butterflies sewn on to the dress. I would use that as a theme and have butterflies on my dress and my bridesmaids' dresses and also have butterfly table decorations.

The more I thought about it, the more excited I became. I couldn't tell Pat, of course, and I wanted to keep the lights a secret from everyone else. It had to be that way, otherwise the impact would be lost when it came to lighting-up time.

I played out the scene in my mind. All would be revealed at the first dance. As the lights dimmed and Pat took me in his arms I would flick a switch and my dress would come to life.

Now all that was needed was a genius to make my dreams come true. Luckily, the traveller community knew just the right person.

Near our home, a short drive away in Liverpool, there was a dress designer called Thelma Madine. She was well known among travellers in the North for her amazing creations. The biggest and best gypsy wedding dresses were Thelma's creations. Her business, Nico Dressmakers, was legendary for the sheer scale and ambition of its creations. Travellers trusted her – they have to trust the people they do business with. So I called Thelma's shop and arranged to go in for a consultation. I panicked that she would not have enough time to make the type of dress I wanted but Thelma reassured me. It would be a tight turnaround but she would be able to do it.

And then there were the bridesmaids' dresses. Pat and I had discussed who we wanted to ask to be bridesmaids. Weddings between non-travellers and travellers were rare and we wanted a mix of bridesmaids to signify that it was two cultures coming together. We chose Chantelle, Pat's cousins Montana, Elycia and Lizzy Marie and my sister-in-law Becky. Well, I call her my sister-in-law but her and Dean never married although they have two children, McKenzie and Kai, and though they have since split up, they are still close and Becky is still part of my family.

I had a special plan for my little sister Tiffany. Although she was only young she had always maintained that she would never get married so I wanted her to be able to wear a wedding dress at least once in her life. She would be a mini-bride. She was going to wear a replica of my dress, without the electronics.

Originally I had planned to have Thelma make the bridesmaids' dresses as well but the more I thought about it, the more I realised that I wanted my dress to stand alone. I didn't want to be upstaged, and as Thelma was such a talent, any of her creations would be a talking point. Instead I decided to have the bridesmaids' dresses made by a corset maker in St Helens. I chose black corset tops with pink piping and lace-up backs. They would be decorated with butterfly motifs to complement the theme of my dress. The skirts would be short, but with pink satin trains flowing to the ground.

A few days after I first called Thelma I went into Liverpool to see her and give her a better idea of the type of design I wanted.

Nico Dressmakers was on the corner of a busy street in the centre of town next to one of Liverpool's big department stores. It looked like any other normal dress shop from the outside. There were a few dresses in the window and part of the shop also sold children's clothes.

Thelma greeted me with her warm Scouse accent and a broad smile. Because she works with so many travellers she was used to dealing with young brides and immediately put me at ease. She was a striking woman with blond hair and a warm charm. She was also a straight-talker. She didn't try to over-impress; her reputation spoke for itself. I could see why travellers liked and respected her. And she was fascinated by my story and the fact that I was a non-traveller marrying into a traveller family.

I told her about the *Coming To America* dress and she ushered me into her office and found the photo I had seen online.

'We can do something like it,' she smiled.

'And I want lights on it,' I said. 'And butterflies.'

'Okay,' she nodded, unfazed by my request.

'But is there any way the butterflies can be different from other ones you have done before?' I asked.

Thelma thought for a moment.

'We can try and do ones that move,' she offered. 'The wings flap, as if they are taking off.'

I gasped. Robotic butterflies *and* lights. That would be amazing.

'How many lights would you want?' she asked.

'Hundreds?' I questioned.

Thelma weighed it up in her mind.

'We can sew threads of LED lights into the fabric,' she said. 'They make them so thin now that it should look like part of the dress. The only thing is that with the lights and the butterflies it might not be that easy hiding the battery packs.'

I hadn't thought about that.

'But if you want a dress that big we should be able to hide them strategically so they don't bulge out and show,' she said.

I got the impression that the more Thelma thought about the dress I was imagining, the more she was relishing the idea of the challenge it posed.

'We can do it,' she stated finally. We were on a tight deadline and the design was a real challenge but Thelma was confident she could create a masterpiece. I felt elated. For someone who used to be a tomboy and hated wearing dresses as a girl, I was now having palpitations thinking about the wedding dress to end all wedding dresses.

Thelma explained the process. She would order in the material, the lights and the butterflies and get to work as soon as they arrived.

'What is your colour scheme?' she asked.

That was a big decision.

'Light pink,' I said.

Pink was not traditional but in traveller culture only girls who had never been with a man were allowed to marry in white. I had thought long and hard about it. I would have loved more than anything to be a virginal white bride but the man who attacked me when I was 11 robbed me of that chance. I knew that if I did choose to walk down the aisle in white I would be lying to myself and to everyone who came to witness our vows. Ultimately I would be lying to God, and I couldn't do that.

Pat understood. I had explained my decision to him. I knew there would be raised eyebrows in the traveller community about my choice of colour but it was a matter of principle. I couldn't start my married life on a lie. We had always been honest with each other and that was what made our relationship as strong as it was. Other people could have their opinions and gossip behind my back: it didn't change how I felt about my man and Pat assured me that it didn't change how he felt about me.

After Thelma had taken down all the details of the dress and measured me up she took me for a look around the factory where she made the dresses. It was in a non-descript warehouse a few minutes' walk from the shop. From the outside it looked like any other industrial unit but inside it was an Aladdin's Cave of treasures.

The walls were lined with rolls and rolls of expensive-looking colourful material. On work benches there were tailor's scissors and sewing machines. Dotted around, mannequins stood, mysterious and silent, with dresses in different stages of production pinned to them. There were artistic sketches and designs pinned to the walls and the whole place felt like something from a fairy tale. I was awestruck.

Thelma explained that sometimes it could take anywhere between four days to four weeks to make a dress and that she often worked through the night to get them ready. Sometimes she would sleep in the factory because she worked such long hours it wasn't worth going home – and I knew this for a fact. I once called her on a Sunday morning and apologised for bothering her on her day off. She laughed and said she was working and had been all the previous night. She usually attended the weddings she made the dresses for and dressed the bride in the morning.

Each of her creations was so intricate it could take hours to get one on and each part of the dress had to go on the bride in a specific order. It was like building a 3-D jigsaw, layer upon layer.

Thelma warned me that the dress I had chosen would be heavy.

'You need to be prepared,' she said. 'There will be a lot of material.'

If it looked as good as I was imagining I was prepared to suffer.

That evening I met up with Pat and although the dress was supposed to be a secret I couldn't hide my excitement. I was fidgeting and dying to tell him.

'What's up with you?' he asked.

'I went to the dress shop today and ordered my dress,' I explained.

'Don't tell me,' he said. 'It's a secret, I don't want to know anything about it.'

It was clever reverse psychology. Pat knew that if ever he wanted to get me to divulge a secret, all he had to do was pretend he didn't want to know. It drove me mad if I thought he wasn't interested.

'But it's amazing,' I said. 'I'm not going to tell you anything about it but it looks a bit like this.' And with that I showed him a photo of the *Coming To America* dress I had saved on my phone.

He laughed hard.

'So now I know what your dress looks like,' he said.

'Ahh, but there is a special surprise,' I said mysteriously. Luckily the wedding was happening soon. I knew there was no way I could keep anything a secret from him for long.

One of the advantages of having a wedding later in the year was that the church we wanted had plenty of availability and we chose the date of 30 October 2010, the day before Halloween. Getting hitched late in the year also meant we had the pick of venues. I started to look at places in and around Earlestown and Haydock. We wanted somewhere close by so that everyone could get to it easily. My family lived locally and although Pat had extended family dotted around the UK, his immediate family all lived in the area. We estimated we would need somewhere big enough to take around 150 people.

After a few phone calls I got in touch with a social club in Haydock. They told me they were free on 30 October and invited me along to have a look around. I went with Mum and the venue looked perfect. It was the right size and had a smart function room where we could have a buffet for the guests. The entrance looked grand with marble flooring and it even had a snooker room, ideal for the men if they decided to wander off and set up camp on their own, as was their custom.

'It's just right for us,' I told the woman in charge of bookings. 'We'll take it.'

With around a month to go before the big day everything was falling into place. I had managed to move the booking for the carriage and we had the church we wanted and the reception venue we wanted. I had heard so many stories of last-minute cancellations and problems with businesses unwilling to do business with travellers that I couldn't believe just how smoothly everything was going.

In fact, it all seemed to be going so smoothly Pat's mum often had to remind me to do the extra things I kept forgetting about.

'Have you ordered the table decorations,' she asked one day.

I hadn't and that night Pat's cousin Elycia and I sat down with the laptop to look for paper butterflies on the Internet.

'What about these?' she cooed, scrolling down the eBay page. 'Or these,' as she clicked on another site.

In the end we must have looked at 400 different paper and foil butterflies. I couldn't believe there were so many different styles.

'That's it,' I huffed. 'I don't care, get any of them. It will be dark anyway, no one will be paying that much attention.'

Away from our wedding plans, Pat and I were busy making arrangements for our new life together. The wedding was just one day; afterwards we started married life properly. Unlike non-travellers who usually moved in with each other first and had a chance to build up their homes, we were starting from nothing. Each weekend we would go into town and buy different things for our new home. Although we had to pay for certain things for the wedding, our families also generously helped out. And friends kept an eye out for anything we could use on their scrap round. It always amazed us that people would throw out perfectly good products just because they replaced them with something new. They would come across electrical goods in perfect working order, bikes with nothing wrong with them and furniture without a mark on it. Pat even found us an oven and a laptop computer. There was nothing wrong with it at all. One day he even turned up at my mum's house with a 60-inch plasma television. Someone had called him and asked him to take it away for scrap.

'I've got you a present,' he laughed.

I made him haul it all the way up the stairs to my room, only to discover that it was far too big to fit anywhere. He had to take it all the way back down again and give it to someone else. As the wedding got nearer, my bottom drawer of household essentials was getting more and more full; all we needed was a trailer to put them all in.

We had planned carefully what we wanted for a new home. The most important thing was a separate bedroom area. We didn't want a trailer where each night we would have to make up a bed. And we didn't want a toilet.

Living space in any trailer is limited so you have to think carefully about layout. Travellers have toilets in the brick sheds they have outside their trailers, so as a rule they don't use toilets inside the trailers. They see it as unclean.

'You cook and eat in the trailer,' Pat explained. 'It's not hygienic to use the toilet next to where you are preparing food.'

It did make sense. Although going to the loo during the winter would be quite cold!

I also stipulated that I didn't want flowers or loud patterns in the seating areas. I had seen so many with horrid brown and green cushions that I just wanted something plain.

While we were looking I realised that just like cars, there are certain makes of trailer that travellers prefer. Older gypsies like Roamers, but on most traveller sites the three makes you would see most of were Tabberts, Hobby and Fendt. Traveller families would also sometimes have a smaller touring caravan for when they went away.

At one sales centre we looked at rows and rows of new and used trailers but none felt like they could be home. Trailers are just like houses; you get a feel for them and when you view them you soon know whether they are right for you or not.

At one sales centre Pat called me over excitedly.

'Come here, Sam, I've found the perfect one,' he called.

I trotted over to a gap between two large new caravans. In the middle of them, Pat was standing outside the oldest, most beat-up caravan I had ever seen. It was tiny, dirty and smeared in grime.

'This is in our price range,' he laughed.

As the days went by I started to worry that we would have nowhere to live after the wedding. We found a trailer that we had our hearts set on but even with Pat's negotiating skills we couldn't it get for the price we wanted to pay. Then we had a stroke of good fortune. A friend of Pat's family had a trailer that he was selling and it was perfect for us. A price was agreed and we had our new home. It was towed on to the Earlestown site, ready for us to move into after we married.

Pat hugged me as we looked at it for the first time. It had a separate bed area, a small kitchen area with a cooker, a gas fire, a dining table and enough bunk space for us and guests to sit on. And there wasn't a floral pattern in site. Finally it seemed that my dreams were coming true.

'It's perfect,' I told him as we busied ourselves moving our stuff into our new home. 'Our first home together.'

I may have been about to leave behind all my creature comforts and the life in a house I had grown up in, but I wasn't nervous. It was a big adventure and I was embarking on it with the man I loved.

# 17

# Bride and Prejudice

It was cold, dark and wet, the type of night where all you want to do is turn on the heating and snuggle up on the sofa in front of the television. The site was quiet except for the occasional bark of a dog.

Inside the trailer, however, there was a party going on. I couldn't believe you could fit so much laughter and warmth in such a small space. The traveller women were holding court and the subject of the evening was my wedding songs.

I hadn't thought about them, I didn't have a clue what to have as our first dance or what piece of music to have playing when I walked down the aisle. But Karen, Chantelle, Elycia and the other women on the site were adamant it had to be the right choice and we had all got together for a glass of wine and a discussion. But because they were traveller women it meant that sometimes the evening became less of a discussion and more of a good-natured argument. Traveller woman have strong views and they like to get their views across.

'What about this,' Chantelle suggested, finding a slow R&B tune on YouTube for everyone to listen to.

'Too modern,' Karen said. 'It's got to be something timeless that means something and will still sound good when you watch the video back in 20 years' time.'

I had not heard half of the songs they were suggesting and many of them were country-and-western ballads, which wasn't really my taste in music. But as the wine kept flowing and the conversation got louder I decided it was probably better to go with the flow. And besides, when I actually listened to the words of some of the songs they were suggesting, I could see what they meant. It was more important to have the first dance to a song that had lyrics that spoke about feelings, rather than one that just had a good tune.

The evening had begun at 7.30 p.m. when we all met up and opened the first bottle of wine. By 1.45 a.m. there were several empty bottles scattered around the kitchen area and we had chosen a grand total of three songs, and one of those was the traditional Wedding March.

But we had found the two most important ones (neither of which I had heard before that night): the songs that would be playing during my first dance with Pat and my dance with my dad. Maybe it was the wine but when I thought about the words in the songs that had been chosen, I felt myself well up.

The first dance with Pat would be to a ballad by Brian McKnight called 'Marry Your Daughter'. I fell in love with one of the lines about a guy marrying his princess.

'Aww, Pat calls me his princess,' I said as I listened to the heartfelt crooning.

And the dance with my dad would be to a song called 'You Can Let Go Now' by a singer called Crystal Shawanda. It was about a daughter saying goodbye to her father at different stages through her life and as soon as I heard it I had a lump in my throat.

Everything was dropping into place. We decided to have a buffet rather than a sit-down meal because at traveller weddings, sometimes guests will turn up unannounced. You cannot be too sure of the exact numbers on the day. I had invited all my extended family. Aunts and uncles who I hadn't seen for years were coming and some old friends got in touch to say they would be there. I was overjoyed to hear that Eddie, my former teacher, would attend. There were a few notable absences, however. One cousin, who I was close to, couldn't come because he was in prison for theft at the time. We told the guests that there would be a camera crew there to film us and this caused a few problems with some of the people on Pat's side of the family.

Travellers are private people and many did not agree with the idea of having a camera crew there as part of a series that would show their traditions and customs. There was also so much prejudice against travellers that several of the men realised that being identified on television could impact on their jobs. When they are touting for work door-to-door, especially if it was for odd jobs or construction work, a traveller would not advertise his heritage for fear of getting the door slammed in his face. So being seen on television might impact adversely.

But we had a rough idea of how many people would attend – around 120 – and the numbers were split evenly between Pat's family and mine. The next hurdle was getting the wedding rings. It had become a hotly debated topic because we could not agree on a common design.

Pat wanted matching rings but wanted his to be a plain band. I didn't want a plain band, I wanted something a bit more unusual. I approached the wedding rings with the same philosophy as I had my dress. As far as I was concerned the ring Pat was going to put on my finger on 30 October was the only wedding ring I would ever wear, so I wanted it to be special.

It didn't matter how much we debated, neither of us

were going to give in. I could understand Pat's point of view, he didn't want a Peter Andre-style blinging band set with diamonds because it would not last five minutes on his scrap round.

In the end we reached a compromise. I chose Pat a plain band from a jeweller's in St Helens and chose my own ring as well – a band with diamonds set all around it which would complement the diamond in my engagement ring.

Because travellers keep finances private it would be disrespectful to divulge how much our wedding actually cost and who paid for what but after the wedding I saw some reports which estimated the day had cost between £100,000 and £150,000. Those figures were hugely exaggerated. It was nowhere near as expensive as that. We paid for the dress and I am sworn to secrecy about how much that was. We also paid for the horse and carriage and the hire of Pat's suit. Initially he had wanted to wear a dark suit with a pink waistcoat and tie to match his best man's and the ushers. His friend Crawford was his best man and Brian and Dean were the ushers. But, as the day drew nearer, and Pat got a better idea of just how extravagant my dress was going to be, he began to reconsider.

'Why don't you wear a white suit?' I told him.

At first he was against the idea. 'It'll look daft,' he argued.

But at the fitting for the pageboys he saw a white suit that he liked. And after he tried it on and saw for himself how good it looked, he fell in love with it.

The rest of the wedding details, like the venue and the three-tiered pink cake with a fairy-tale castle on top, were given as gifts. Travellers are hugely generous and both my family and Pat's family all chipped in to help make our special day as perfect as we wanted it to be.

We didn't have a wedding list, that isn't customary for travellers, and they don't give money or vouchers, they buy presents. We already had everything we needed for our trailer and it would have been pointless asking for loads more items for the home because there would not have been enough space to store anything. We didn't need chairs and sofas and all those gadgets that you can buy for the kitchen because the trailer already came with its own built-in furniture. Travellers only need to buy furniture if they have chalets or build bungalows and even then they are smaller than most homes so they do not need to buy lots of stuff. You rarely see travellers in IKEA! If they need new furniture they will most likely go to independent shops where they can negotiate a better price.

A few weeks before the big day I started to think about a special surprise for Pat; some kind of gift that I could give him to show my appreciation for everything he and his family had done for me, and how much I loved him. At that point no one had thought about how he was going to get to the church. He was staying in a posh hotel in Haydock the night before the wedding and I didn't want him to have to get to the church in a van. I had heard of other traveller grooms using all kinds of vehicles to get to their weddings. Some hired sports cars, some hired stretch limousines and I had heard of one who took a helicopter flight. Given the short distance between Haydock and the church, and the lack of helicopter landing pads in Earlestown, I decided a chopper would have been impractical. So I started looking online for something special that Pat could have fun with on the wedding morning.

After a few minutes I found just what I was looking for – a huge red limousine Monster Truck. I grinned as I read the details. It had a champagne bar, a dance floor with a pole in it, digital surround sound, a 50-inch plasma screen with seven additional screens to show pop videos on and lasers and strobe lights. And they threw in a free bottle of bubbly.

'Perfect,' I giggled and called straight away and booked it. I had my glass carriage; Pat had his Monster Truck.

I planned two hen nights. I didn't have enough time to organise a big trip to somewhere like Blackpool and so decided to go to a few local pubs and clubs on both occasions. The first hen night was for the older members of our close family; mums, grans and aunts. It was a sober affair and a good opportunity for both sides of the family to meet before the big day. It is unusual for gypsy girls to be on their own without men and often, if they do attend an event outside the site, an older male member of the family will go along and stay in the background, acting like a chaperone and making sure nothing untoward happens. John Thomas came and sat on the other side of the bar to keep an eye on things on my hen night.

My other hen night was for the younger ones, friends and cousins. Even though the unmarried girls were not allowed to drink, it didn't stop them having a good time and it didn't stop me having too much to drink. We all looked fab in our party gear as we danced our way through the pubs in nearby Ashton but after a few hours I began to feel woozy.

'I've got to go outside,' I told my sister-in-law Becky as I swayed towards the front door.

The bouncers sniggered as I stumbled outside. The cold air hit me like a sledgehammer and my head started spinning.

'Oh God,' I moaned as I leaned against a wall. After a few minutes I wobbled back to the door but the bouncers blocked my way.

'Sorry, love,' they said. 'You've had too much to drink, we're not letting you back in.'

I didn't have a phone on me and had no way of contacting anyone so I staggered home on my own, barred from my own hen night.

Like me, Pat had his stag do in the local pubs. He didn't fare much better. He ended up getting in a drunken argument with some of his friends. They started to play fight and staggered into a thorn bush. He spent the early hours plucking thorns from his arms and side and ruined one of his favourite T-shirts.

With just under a week to go before the wedding Pat realised he had not even seen the venue so we decided to take a trip to it to have another look around. We called up and the helpful receptionist told us to come whenever we wanted.

'You'll love it,' I told Pat as I made the five-minute drive.

We were greeted at the door by an elderly member of staff. There were hardly any people there, just a few old men drinking pints at the bar.

'They'll be glad of the business this time of year,' I said to Pat as we planned who would sit where in the function room.

The person showing us around seemed to take an unusual interest in Pat and asked him lots of questions about the wedding. She even asked what Pat did for a living, which I thought was odd at the time but assumed she was just being polite.

After a quick look around Pat was satisfied I had made the right choice and we left.

The following day my phone rang. I didn't recognise the number.

'Is that Miss Norton?' a woman's voice asked nervously.

I told her it was.

'I'm calling from the wedding reception venue, you are booked in with us next Saturday. I'm afraid I have some bad news.'

My heart sank. *What now?* I thought. *I bet there's been a problem with the caterers.*

'We cannot take your booking,' she said. 'We are going to have to cancel it.'

Her words did not register at first. I had to ask her to repeat herself.

She explained that our booking had been discussed by

the committee that runs the club and they had decided to cancel it.

'Why?' I asked, anger rising. But I already knew the answer.

'We don't host traveller weddings,' she said apologetically.

'But… but… it's less than a week to go and it's the night before Halloween, everywhere else will have parties planned, how am I going to find another venue at such late notice?'

But it was no good, I knew there was no hope in trying to argue with her, so I gave her a piece of my mind before hanging up in tears.

The worst thing was I should have expected it. It had all been too easy. Pat had warned me that a huge number of traveller weddings get cancelled because the venues find out beforehand that the guests will be travellers. They have a bad reputation and posh venues panic and think that they will be overrun with aggressive, drunk hooligans. Never mind that the huge majority of traveller weddings go off without problems and there are just as many drunken brawls at non-traveller weddings. There is a deep mistrust of travellers when they congregate in one place. I had already experienced the prejudice on a smaller scale being followed around shops by security guards when I was with Pat. They just knew by looking at him that he was a traveller and that is what had happened when we went to look at the venue.

'Why did you have to come with me?' I cried, when I called him to tell him the news.

'They would have found out one way or another,' he reasoned. 'Maybe it's better finding out now than turning up on the day and being sent away?'

'But I can't understand what we're supposed to do, Pat. Do people expect you to announce who you are whenever you go somewhere? You wouldn't expect black people or Asian people to have to do that, it's racist.'

'It's just the way people are, Princess,' he sighed.

It took another two days of frantic phone calls until we finally found an alternative venue: the Grove Social Club in St Helens. They were happy to have us and luckily they did not have any parties booked.

Despite the fiasco surrounding the venue, everything else had fallen into place and with just a day to go before the wedding I had one more thing to do. And this was something I knew I was going to enjoy. My dress was ready and it was time for the fitting.

Over the weeks I had been in constant contact with Thelma and each time I phoned to find out how she was progressing she got me more and more excited.

'Oh Sam,' she'd say, 'it's looking amazing. I think it's one of the best ones I've done.'

I took Mum and Tiffany to the fitting and as we walked up to the shop the butterflies swirling in my stomach were as big and numerous as the ones I hoped would be on my dress.

Thelma greeted us with a grin and beckoned us inside. I could tell she was just as eager as we were. It was dim in the shop and Thelma led us to a room at the back. The door was shut and she lined us up in front of it.

'Are you ready for this?' she smiled.

I nodded eagerly and she flung open the door. It was like opening the door to Santa's grotto, the lights seemed to fill the room. The dress was on a stand fully lit up. The crystals sparkled in the light and the 21 butterflies gently flapped their wings. With yards and yards of material and hundreds of lights and crystals it looked like the room was full of clouds and snowflakes.

I was expecting something special but had never in my wildest dreams imagined something so spectacular. My mouth was wide open but I couldn't find any words to describe what I felt. Instead I just squealed.

I had a tiny worry at the back of my mind that the dress would be too over-the-top, even slightly tacky. I needn't have worried. It was amazing.

I felt someone nudging me. I had been in shock staring at it, so engrossed that I forgot I was with other people. Mum was screaming and crying and Thelma was asking 'Do you like it, Sam?'

I nodded, still overwhelmed by the sight of this extraordinary, beautiful dress.

'I can't believe it,' I whispered emotionally. 'It's better than I could have ever imagined.'

There was more to come. Thelma showed me Tiffany's dress and again I was amazed. It was a perfect replica except for the lights and moving butterflies.

Mum continued to cry. I think that was the first time it suddenly hit her that her little girl was getting married.

That night would be my last as a single woman, but I'd been part of a couple for what seemed like so long that single life wasn't something I mourned. I couldn't wait to start married life and to become Pat's wife. It would be a big adventure: it wasn't just a wedding, I was leaving home and going to live in a totally new culture. I was excited, and a little nervous.

But underneath the nerves there was a sense of calm. What I was doing felt right – I was nervous in the way that a performer feels nervous before stepping on to a stage. Tomorrow I would be the centre of attention, and something could go wrong – my dress might not light up in the way I wanted it to, I could trip and fall, ruining the effect, Pat's truck could break down on the way to the church. But underlying those fears was the absolute certainty that what I was doing was right. Pat was wonderful, and he treated me wonderfully, like a princess, not the namby-pamby Disney version, but the real flesh-and-blood kind, the princess of his heart. And his family had been so warm and welcoming, they had helped me learn their traditions and had shown me what it was like to be part of a community that looked after and cared for its members. I had to stop from pinching myself at times – I felt incredibly lucky to be joining such an amazing group of people.

I often wondered where I would be if I hadn't met up with Pat again. I'd probably still be angry and lashing out at my family, probably would be in a dead-end job that I hated, probably would be going out with my friends and meeting boys that I had no interest in pursuing a relation-ship with. And the worst thing is that I wouldn't know what I was missing. I wouldn't know how sad I was because I hadn't experienced the happiness that I had found with Pat. Pat and his family had saved me and I was soon going to have something that money can't buy: a place in a vibrant and welcoming community and the kind of stability that had been missing from my life ever since my parents split up – and all because I had the love of a man whom I loved with all my heart.

I went to have my nails done – long, pink and crystal-tipped to match my dress – and then went back to Mum's for my last night of living inside a house. Pat was staying at the hotel and had gone out for a few nerve-steadying drinks with his all-male wedding party. As I drifted off to sleep I imagined fairy-tale carriages and butterflies, and my Prince Charming coming to carry me away.

# 18

# I Do

The sound of crying echoed up the stairs; my first memory of my wedding day.

Blinking in the light I looked at the clock: 7 a.m. My wedding day had finally arrived. And somewhere in the house all hell was breaking loose.

'It's broken,' I could hear my sis Tiffany sobbing.

I slipped on my dressing gown and went downstairs to see what the fuss was about. In the lounge Tiffany was pointing a crushed tiara accusingly at my mum. It had snapped. Apparently Mum had accidently trodden on it the night before.

I took a deep breath.

'Don't worry, Tiff, you can wear Mum's,' I told her, shooting my Mum a look. It was going to be a long day and this wasn't the best start. But a few protracted negotiations later Tiffany was calmed down. The first disaster of the day had been averted.

I looked out the front window and smiled. The sky was clear and the winter sun was shining.

Across town in a hotel room somewhere, my husband-to-be was waking up and I imagined what he was feeling. Was he as nervous as me? I didn't know it at the time but Pat had already had his own drama. His quiet pre-wedding drinks had turned into a boozy night after the kindly barman gave him a whole bottle of Aftershock to celebrate his impending nuptials. At some point in the evening there was a fight, which he wasn't involved in, but the police arrived and Pat had to talk his way out of being taken in for questioning. They let him go because he explained that he was getting hitched the following day.

After a quick cup of tea I hurriedly threw on some clothes and made my way to the hairdresser's for my eight o'clock appointment. I was wearing my hair down and it had to be perfect as I was wearing a long chiffon veil and a beautiful crystal tiara as big as a crown. I started to make a mental list of what I needed to do: hair, make-up, put on dress, get married. I needed to be at the church by one o'clock so I had plenty of time and enjoyed the quiet in the hairdresser's. It would be the last bit of peace I had that day.

When I got back to Mum's the house was crowded with friends and relations. The bridesmaids had arrived and were starting to get ready and Mum had opened the wine.

The house continued to fill with neighbours and well-wishers and after a while it seemed as though an impromptu party had broken out. Tiffany was taking her duties as a mini-bride extremely seriously and following me wherever I went. I could feel myself getting increasingly anxious. I had wanted a relaxing morning but it was turning into a knees-up. After an hour, with my hair done and fully made up I walked out to the corner shop just to get some space. *Calm down, Sam*, I told myself, *everyone is just excited*. After a few deep breaths I went back just as Thelma arrived in her car with the dress.

You couldn't see through the back window because of all the material. It took two people to carry it into the house and people passing by were stopping to look at the seemingly never-ending procession of billowing pink material being ferried through the front door. We set aside a room where Thelma and her two assistants could dress me. We had 90 minutes before I needed to be at the altar. *Plenty of time*, I thought to myself.

But getting into a dress as big as mine was no easy feat. Thelma asked me what I was wearing on my feet. I showed her the dainty wedding heels I had bought.

She shook her head.

'You won't be able to wear those,' she said. 'The heels will snap in half within minutes.'

*Oh my God*, I thought, *just how heavy* is *the dress?*

Thelma explained that although it hadn't been weighed, as an estimate the entire dress complete with lights, butter-flies and battery packs would be around 20 stone.

'That'll be like carrying my dad on my back all day!' I exclaimed.

As the heels were a definite no-no, there was another last-minute problem. The dress was measured to fit my height in heels; without them it would be several inches too long. But it was too late in the day to start making alterations so I hunted through my wardrobe for a pair of shoes with the thickest soles I could find. I settled on a pair of black Ugg boots.

'At least you'll be comfortable,' Thelma laughed.

She had already given me a crash course in how to wear the dress and warned me about the dangers. It was not like putting on a normal dress. I knew it could cut so deeply into my hips it would leave scars. Many girls didn't protect themselves against these injuries and wore their scars with pride. I didn't want to injure myself, so rather than wearing traditional bridal lingerie I padded myself out with three pairs of tummy tuck shorts and wrapped my midriff in bandages.

I felt like the Michelin Man and although it wasn't sexy, at least I knew I wouldn't spend the day in agony.

The dressing process started with a frame – a skirt with hoops in it that would push the material off my legs. Then came the underskirts. There were 21 of them, and each one was made up of five separate pieces of material. I had to stand through the whole process and slipped on underskirt after underskirt while Thelma and her assistants burrowed around underneath me making sure they were all secured properly and lined up in the right order while they wired in the lights and expertly hid the battery packs. The room seemed to get smaller and smaller as I got bigger – I felt like Alice in Wonderland standing there in my bra. I laughed when I realised it would be many hours before I saw my feet again.

The house was a buzz of activity. I heard my dad arrive and called out to say hello to him.

'Don't come in,' I shouted, 'you need to see it when it's finished.'

In another room Tiffany was getting into her dress. Mum was desperately trying to keep her indoors as a crowd of onlookers had started to gather outside and if Tiffany went out, everyone would know what my dress looked like.

Word had started to spread through town that there was a big wedding taking place and people wanted to see what all the fuss was about.

Then I heard the clip-clop of a horse's hooves in the road outside.

I gasped. 'What's the time?' I said.

It was 12.30 p.m. I felt hot and prickly; I was only half dressed and was going to be late.

'Don't you worry,' Thelma reassured me. 'You're the bride, it's your day. They'll have to wait for you.'

I calmed myself down and stepped into another underskirt.

Meanwhile across town Pat had just climbed into his Monster Truck with Crawford, Crawford's son Ricardo, Dean, Brian, John Thomas and Levi.

They had the vehicle for an hour with a driver and cracked open a few beers, put on some music and headed off down the motorway for a joyride. Pat had spent the morning organising the boys and arranging the last-minute details with the DJ.

My phone beeped and I read the message and smiled. *Thanks for the truck, see you at the altar,* it said.

By now all the skirts were finally on. I had 105 pieces of material billowing from my waist. Then came the satin and crystal-studded bodice, the sleeves with puff-ball pink chiffon shoulders, the tiara and the flowing veil. The dress was made of separate pieces and once they had all been assembled together it was a masterpiece. My heart was pounding when I looked in the mirror. I couldn't recognise the woman looking back at me. She looked like she had been plucked from the pages of a fairy tale.

Thelma and her assistants helped me out into the front room where Dad saw me in my wedding dress for the first time. I could see his eyes well up as he swallowed back his emotions.

'You look beautiful, Sam,' he smiled.

Mum was dressed by then too. She had bought a beautiful pink dress for the wedding and had added a black lacy train to it and wore elbow-length black gloves.

'I had to add some accessories when I realised how extravagant your dress was going to be,' she said.

Finally we were all ready. I glanced at the clock. We were an hour late.

'Will you be able to get out the door?' Dad asked.

I hadn't thought about that but Thelma helped inch me out and lifted the hems of the dress to stop them catching under my feet.

'You look amazing, Sam,' she said. 'This will be the best day of your life.'

Outside it seemed as if the whole street had turned out to see me. There were people lined up at the front wall taking photos and videos as I waddled out of the front door.

'I feel like a celebrity,' I giggled as I gingerly crossed the garden. The carriage was waiting on the road outside. I had only seen photographs of it before and it looked more magical in real life than I imagined. Ornate and dainty, with two smartly dressed grooms and a beautiful white steed wearing a plumed headpiece, it was perfect.

Thelma carefully helped me in and packed the dress around me while Dad found a space and sat opposite. By now the traffic was backing up along the road and we were followed by a line of well-wishers hooting horns as we made our way to the church.

By the time we arrived I was 90 minutes late and as I looked around for a friendly face I didn't recognise anyone. The Monster Truck had already drawn a crowd and complete strangers were snapping away as I got out of the carriage. Nervously, I made my way to the front door and met my bridesmaids who all looked amazing. By then the nerves had really started to take effect and I was also beginning to realise just how heavy the dress was. Each step was an effort and I had to keep shifting uncomfortably to stop my back from aching. Dad squeezed my hand but the dress was so wide he had to reach over to do it.

Inside the church I heard the first bars of the Wedding March pipe through the sound system.

'Are you ready, Sam?' Dad asked.

I looked at him and my eyes filled with tears.

'I can't do it, Dad,' I said, wedding nerves suddenly biting.

'You'll be fine, darling,' he smiled. 'I'm with you every step of the way.'

I started walking towards my future and as I walked through the doors I saw a handsome vision in white waiting by the altar. Pat, my husband-to-be. He looked gorgeous. He turned and our eyes met. His face lit up and an invisible thread of love pulled me towards him. It was hard to walk with so much material and so much weight and Dad was having trouble not stepping on the trailing fabric but I didn't even notice. I just focused on Pat and all my nerves and anxiety dissolved away. Even when one of the bridesmaids stepped on my veil, which was trailing on the ground, and nearly yanked it off I didn't flinch. I quickly readjusted it and continued forward.

I allowed myself a quick look around. There was Mum in the front, and Karen and Pat's dad. I saw my brothers and aunts and uncles, all looking amazing in their posh outfits. At the back of the church there were even strangers from the neighbourhood who had snuck inside the church to witness our wedding. One of them was still in her pyjamas. I didn't realise how much of a stir our wedding had caused.

As I stood alongside Pat he looked at me and mouthed the words, 'You're beautiful.'

The vicar began to recite the vows and I followed every word, repeating mine with all the sincerity I had in my heart.

'I do,' I said, gazing into Pat's eyes. At that moment there was just him and me – everyone else disappeared into the background.

When Pat slipped the ring on my finger I felt my heart burst.

'I now pronounce you man and wife,' the vicar exclaimed.

He didn't say, 'You may now kiss the bride.' He didn't have to. Pat leaned across the yards of fabric that separated us and tenderly kissed my lips.

'My husband,' I whispered. The congregation cheered and whistled.

After the ceremony we planned to light candles of remembrance but one of the church officials warned that it would be safer if I stayed away from naked flames.

'You've only got to brush against a lit candle and that dress will go up like a firework,' she advised.

She was right: it was an accident waiting to happen. We decided to leave the candle lighting for another day.

Outside the church Pat stood back to admire my dress. 'Sam, it's amazing,' he said.

Thelma came over to congratulate us. 'She looks beautiful,' she told Pat. 'You look after her, you're a very lucky man.'

'I know and I intend to,' he smiled.

By the time we got into the carriage, cars filled with guests and onlookers were lined up behind, ready to follow us to the venue. There must have been over 100 and as we wound our way through the streets people came out of their houses to see what all the fuss was about. We giggled and waved at them.

'It's like a Royal Wedding,' I laughed. Pat was a gypsy prince and I was his princess.

Halfway to the venue Pat called out to the driver to pull over at a Spar shop we were passing.

'I'm so thirsty,' he said and jumped out of the carriage to buy a can of Red Bull. My mouth was dry too, partly because of the nerves and partly due to the fact that I had decided I wasn't going to drink anything that day if I could help it. There were certain technical difficulties associated with my dress and one of them was what would happen if I needed the loo.

Thelma had explained that if and when the urge took me I would have to get her and my bridesmaids and they would have to come in the cubicle with me and hold the dress up. And because I couldn't reach underneath it someone would have to wipe me!

I decided at that point I wouldn't be using the loo and so there would be no booze throughout the day, which was ironic, considering that in the eyes of some of the more traditional travellers as I was now married I was, under traveller rules, allowed to have a drink.

When Pat got back in the carriage, cars had started passing us and some were hooting. Although most of them were cheering, a few had some choice words for us, obviously annoyed at being held up.

'You look like a couple of t**ts,' one man screamed out of his car window. Pat launched his empty can at the heckler and narrowly missed him as he pulled his head back inside the car and sped off.

When we got to the venue the guests were already filing in and tucking into the buffet. Pat had gone in ahead but Thelma needed to make a few dress adjustments. Pat came back out and grabbed my hand to lead me in.

'I can't move,' I told him. 'There are three people under the dress.'

'Don't lie,' he laughed.

I wasn't. Up until that point Pat hadn't realised just how big the dress was. He lifted the hem and bent down for a look. Thelma and her assistants waved out at him.

For most of the rest of the day I remained seated. I realised how immobile I was after I sat down on the floor for some pictures with the dress billowing out around me. I couldn't stand back up. Pat tried to pull me up but couldn't, then my dad came to help and needed a few others as well. I felt like an enormous turnip with a line of people trying to tug me from the ground.

We didn't have a sit-down meal so there were no traditional speeches, although Pat said a few words and thanked the guests. I decided to say something too. Getting to my feet I turned to him and said, 'As long as I have you in my life I never need to ask for anything else. Everything I need is standing here in front of me.'

At that moment I felt like the luckiest girl alive.

Later I had my first dance with my dad and after keeping my emotions together the tears finally began to flow. I think that was when it hit me. I was leaving my old life; I belonged to another man.

After a reapplication of mascara it was time for my big surprise. Thelma guided me into a side room and began the process of switching on each component. One by one sections of the dress lit up and the butterflies, that had sat patiently all day waiting for their moment, started to move, slowly flapping their wings in time with my breath.

'They're all working,' Thelma said. She stood back, looked at her creation and beamed. Then she turned serious.

'Now, Sam, you must come and tell me if any part of the dress starts to feel hot or if you smell smoke,' she said, fixing my gaze.

I frowned. 'Are you joking?' I said.

She pulled a small red fire extinguisher from her handbag and shook her head. 'I'm probably just being paranoid but there are a lot of battery packs in there, I don't want any of them to overheat.'

Outside the guests were wondering what was happening as the lights had been dimmed in the room ready for my entrance.

There were gasps as I walked out. Some guests just stared mutely, transfixed by the lights glowing like an aura around me.

'Let's have a round of applause for the first dance,' announced the DJ. I scanned the crowd. Where was Pat?

Karen ran off to find him and I breathed in deeply to calm my nerves.

Through the crowd I saw my husband making his way towards me. He was my very own white knight. He stopped in his tracks in front of me, mouth slightly open. His eyes looked me lovingly up and down, drinking me in.

'Wow,' he mouthed.

'It's our first dance,' I whispered.

We couldn't get too close. The dress was a soft, puffy barrier between us. Pat had to lean across it but I didn't care. At that point I was lost in his outstretched arms and lost in the music.

I hadn't noticed before but when I looked around, I realised that the men and women were all sitting and standing together, not separately like at most of the traveller functions I had been to. In fact, once the cameras went, everyone mixed in together, gypsies and non-travellers. I wondered if it was the start of a thaw between communities. Why did there have to be distrust on both sides? I hoped that maybe there were some guests there who may have started the day with fixed opinions and prejudices about the other community but finished it without them. After all, underneath it didn't matter what your background was or where you came from, ultimately we were all humans.

The rest of the night went without a hitch. The two communities laughed and danced and there was just one minor scuffle started by a non-traveller who had drunk too much. In the general scheme of weddings, it was nothing.

The traveller girls who attended had all made a huge effort with their outfits and looked amazing. I didn't see any grabbing and as the guests started to leave many of them told Pat and I that it had been the best wedding they had ever been to.

The day passed in a blur but it will be a day I'll never forget. As the last guests left and Pat and I prepared for our first night as man and wife I found it hard to believe that so many hours ago I was waking up to the sound of Tiffany and Mum arguing. In some ways it seemed as though the day had passed in the blink of an eye; in others it seemed like another lifetime ago.

My life had changed in a day. Tomorrow I would begin a new one in a new, strange environment.

That night Pat and I stayed at a local hotel. Thankfully it took a lot less time getting out of my dress than it did getting into it. As I peeled off layer after layer the hotel room filled up with material until it felt as though we were wading through cotton clouds. We tried to stuff as much of it as we could into the wardrobe, just to make some space for ourselves.

By that time my feet, legs and back were aching so much I could barely walk. I stood in front of the mirror and looked at my back. The small of it was markedly more inwardly curved than it had been in the morning – a permanent effect and to this day I still have a sway back. I didn't get scars on my hips but my dress did leave its mark after all.

Once it was all off I walked round the room and I felt weightless, like an astronaut walking on the moon.

I sat on the bed and reflected on the day. I was now a married woman and I vowed to be a good wife and to look after Pat, to love and care for him, to cook and clean for him and to support him. That was the contract I had entered into. I would never be a full-blooded traveller but I would try to be something like a traveller wife. In return I knew that Pat would protect me and provide for me. It might not have been everyone's idea of how a marriage should be but it was how I wanted my marriage.

That night we were both too exhausted to do what most newly-weds do. That would have to wait. The day had drained us and it didn't help that I had spent most of it with 20 stone hanging off my back. Instead, for the first time in my life, I snuggled up to the man I loved and fell asleep in his arms. Finally we were allowed to be together as a proper couple and to share ourselves. I drifted off into a peaceful sleep with a smile on my lips, knowing that in the morning the first thing I would see would be his beautiful face.

# 19

## A Dutiful Wife

The huge electric gates hummed and rolled back across the entrance. Pat put the van in gear and inched forward into the courtyard. It was quiet, there were no children playing, curtains were pulled.

We were home at last and I was embarking on the first day of my new life. I was a non-traveller in a gypsy world and wondered how well I'd adapt.

I looked over to Pat. He must have read my mind.

'We're going to be so happy here, Princess,' he said, squeezing my thigh.

We pulled up outside our trailer. It was shiny and clean: a new home for a new beginning. I couldn't quite believe we finally had our own space, somewhere we could settle.

Someone had pinned a 'congratulations' banner across the door.

Pat took my hand and led me to the threshold.

'I'd carry you in but the door is too narrow for two people,' he laughed.

He was right, I would have to get used to our trailer's new proportions. After a house I worried it would be cramped. There was no upstairs, no front and back garden and hardly any storage space. But it didn't matter.

'I'd live in a bin if it meant I could be with you,' I told Pat.

I took a moment to look around and Pat stood behind me with his hands on my shoulders. A thought suddenly struck me. I had known him since I was 11 years old and had grown up with him in my life. But this was the first time I was alone with him in a trailer. Finally it felt like our love was sanctioned.

I still had things to learn, I still had to get used to day-to-day life on the site, but at least I could be a wife to my husband and be alone with him without eyebrows being raised. It felt weird. Our entire relationship had been carried out in front of other people, in public places. But finally we were alone, just the two of us. What were we supposed to do?

'Shall I put the kettle on?' I asked.

I had to get used to the fact that a gypsy wife should always look after her husband and make sure that his needs are met.

'Yes, please,' said Pat.

I automatically walked over to the kitchen area and reached across the work surface for the kettle. It wasn't there. Neither was the tap. I'd forgotten that the kettle was in the brick shed outside and that was where the drinks were made.

I giggled and walked past Pat and outside into the cold. Inside the shed – which is actually more like a utility room – we had a cooker, a washing machine, a fridge and a separate toilet area. There was a microwave and a smaller cooker inside the trailer and I planned to use those if it was raining or exceptionally cold. There were logistics to work out for my new way of life and I realised as I stood in the shed making the tea that I would have to learn on the job, trial and error.

During our first day back I offered to cook but we went for a meal instead, then lazed around on the bunks watching television and chatting about the previous day. We had a pile of wedding presents to open but decided to do that the following day.

'What shall we do tonight?' Pat wondered.

I suddenly remembered that it was Halloween.

'There's a fancy dress party on in the pub?' I suggested.

And that was how we spent our first day as a married couple. The previous night when I was undressing I had thought to myself that I wouldn't care if I never put on another dress in my life. But less than 24 hours later I was scrambling around trying to find another outrageous frock to wear to a party.

Luckily I had a perfect orange-and-black number in the wardrobe at Mum's and we drove to pick it up. That was another thing I would have to get used to: there wasn't enough space in the trailer for all my stuff and I had clothes stored at Mum's and Dad's. I'd have to keep a check on where everything was. For Pat it was easier, he had grown up in trailers and so hadn't had the opportunity to accumulate loads and loads of stuff. The first consideration for a traveller when they buy something is 'Have I got room for it?' They live light.

That night I back-combed my hair, got made up again and we went out. The one concession I did make was to wear boots rather than heels. My back and legs were still sore from wearing the dress the previous day.

Over the next few days we gradually settled into married life. We spent a fun afternoon opening our presents and proudly displayed all the ornaments and collectables we were given. Gypsies are just as generous with their wedding presents as they are over-the-top with their wedding outfits. They don't try to find the cheapest option, they go for the expensive things. But their gifts are not what non-travellers would call practical. You won't get a toaster from a gypsy.

They buy presents that will hold their price and retain sentimental value. Crystal ornaments and expensive tableware are the traveller gift of choice. And the more luxurious the brand, the better. Just like designer clothes, there were some makes of ornament that were prized over others.

Pat's nan taught me the basics. She bought us a beautiful set of porcelain plates. We also had a ceramic dog inlaid with 24-carat gold, a china dinner set and several Waterford crystal ornaments to dot proudly around the trailer.

Pat's nan told me to put our best china out on display and use the rest to eat off. I was scared to use it and was forever worrying that I'd knock something over. Soon after we got married I was putting up some plates and one slipped and smashed. I managed to glue it back together but was horrified at what I had accidentally done.

Travellers value collectables because they know that should they ever need money, they have things they can sell. Our gifts were like insurance policies for the future, they were there to display in the good times but could act as security if we fell on hard times.

Travellers can also be creative when it comes to giving

gifts. Pat and his family once considered buying Pat's nephew an alpaca as a Christmas present, rather than a normal pet such as a cat or a dog. They went to look at one but the owner explained that the animals should be kept in pairs and so the family decided it may not have been such a good idea after all.

After our first idyllic days together as husband and wife, the time came for Pat to go back to work. Huddled under the duvet, I heard him creaking around the trailer, getting dressed. I heard the click of the gas fire ignition and smiled. He was turning on the heating for me so it would be warm when I got out of bed.

Climbing out of bed I crept over to him and put my arms around him.

'I'll miss you, babe,' I whispered.

It would be strange not having him there with me. I was nervous about the first day on my own at the site. I kissed him goodbye and waved him off and was alone for the first time. Even though his mum, sister and nan lived just a few trailers away I felt suddenly isolated. The site is very different in the daytime when all the men leave to go to work. Each morning a procession of cars and vans leave and once they are gone the site becomes very quiet. And because it is not a big site, there are not lots of children there to break the silence.

I knew there were people around me if I needed them. Pat was always just a call or text away and on each site there is someone in charge who makes sure things run properly. On our site it was Pat's uncle Jack. I knew I wasn't alone, but I felt nervous all the same. What was I supposed to do? There is no *How to be a Traveller's Wife* manual. You learn through watching the others and I knew the most important task of the day was the cleaning.

Most traveller men will not lift a finger around the house unless it is to fix something, they don't go out and do the shopping, some will not even make themselves a cup of tea. But Pat was different. He would cook and make a drink for himself and he would go shopping with me and insist on carrying the bags. I thought he might change after we married but he didn't. However, even though I was lucky enough to have a progressive, modern-thinking hubby, I wanted to care for him and look after him. I wanted to make sure when he came home the trailer was clean for him and there was dinner waiting.

So I set about my cleaning duties.

To begin with I loved cleaning. It was a novelty, as I had never had a home of my own to clean. And there was a routine to cleaning a trailer. First I pulled up the mats on the floor and shook them outside, then I cleaned all the floors. Travellers don't use mops, they get on their hands and knees with a cloth because that is the only way you can guarantee to get a thorough cleanse. Then I cleaned the cushions on the bunks and wiped down the surfaces and cleaned the inside windows.

I learned the practicalities of trailer living. There was no hot water inside so to do the washing up I had to boil a kettle and pour the water in a bowl. The lack of hot water meant no shower or bath and so most days I would go home to my mum's, which wasn't ideal. I couldn't have a nice bath at night and then put my pyjamas on and get into bed. I would have a bath and then get changed back into my clothes and go home. Travellers not lucky enough to have family nearby would use the facilities at the local leisure centre where it cost £1.50 for a shower.

On some big council-run sites they have bath houses, but the rental there was as much as a house then you have to pay gas plus electricity and water. Living as a traveller was not as cheap as many people believed.

I also learned through bitter experience to secure the trailer when I went out. Normally you can leave a window open or a door unlocked because you can trust your neighbours. But you can't trust the weather and when I left the skylights open one day I returned to find the trailer flooded after a rainstorm. It took hours to clean up and dry out.

Over the weeks our lives settled into the rhythm of marriage. We still made sure we went on dates. Every Wednesday we would go to the pictures and often on the weekend we would go out for a meal.

On cold nights we'd snuggle on the sofa and watch television. On Sundays I would cook a roast and we'd sit at the table and eat.

Although I loved those first weeks of married life, I would be lying if I said it wasn't hard. It was a particularly cold winter. Mornings were freezing and it was a struggle to get out of bed when outside everything was caked in a layer of ice and snow.

And there was another issue with living in a trailer that I had not anticipated, something deeper and more psychological. I began to have anxiety attacks. I developed an irrational fear of intruders. There was a deep-seated insecurity that had been under control all the time I lived in a house. But in the trailer I felt exposed. I no longer had a solid front door to lock behind me. I didn't have the security of bricks and mortar. Even though the huge electric gates at the only entrance to the site meant it was practically impossible for strangers to wander in I still worried about getting attacked. Our trailer was at the far end of the courtyard and was bordered by a low wire-mesh fence that separated the trailer park from the railway line that ran alongside it. I convinced myself that it would have been easy for an intruder to climb over.

Even when I was with Pat at night I would sometimes work myself up into a state of terror, convinced there were prowlers outside.

'Is the door locked, babe?' I asked for the tenth time while we lay in bed one evening.

'Yes,' he sighed.

'Can you get up and check again, please?' I begged.

No matter how much he reassured me that we were safe and secure and that he wouldn't let anything happen to me, I still fretted.

If I needed to go to the loo in the night I would lie there holding it in until it got light, too scared to step outside in the dark on my own.

Pat, as ever, was patient and understanding and over time the fear subsided but never completely went away.

Although I loved my new home and my new life, after a while I decided to go back to work in the pub. The money would come in handy and sometimes days on my own in the trailer would pass slowly. Pat was happy with the idea. Many traveller men would not agree with their women working, but Pat was much more open-minded.

However, although initially it felt good to be out at work, I started to realise that I was seeing less and less of my husband, and we'd only been married a few weeks. He would leave at eight in the morning, and I would be at work when he came home. I began to feel guilty about not being there for him and not having his dinner ready for when he came home at night, so eventually I gave up work and went back to the day-to-day routine of cleaning and cooking. I began to realise how invaluable the slow cooker was that Karen had given me months before. I'd learnt that traditional cheap cuts like brisket and shin of beef were perfect for putting into warming stews and took little time to prepare. You could leave them on a low heat in the pot all day, filling the trailer with an enticing aroma as it cooked.

As those early weeks went by we began to plan for our first Christmas together. I wanted it to be as special as possible and, in honour of my dress, which by then was unceremoniously dumped in a box in my old room at Mum's, I decided on a special tree.

'I want a pink one,' I explained to Pat.

There wasn't loads of room in the trailer and we couldn't have a big six-foot tree but we were definitely going to have something more substantial than a table-top effort.

'They have them at ASDA, I've seen them advertised on TV,' I continued.

The next day we drove ten miles to the nearest ASDA, only to discover there were no pink trees in stock.

'How about this one,' Pat tried, gesturing to a silver tinsel tree.

'It's got to be pink,' I insisted.

The store called other branches to check availability and eventually found one in Wigan that had the pink trees I wanted in stock.

'We'll get it tomorrow,' said Pat.

'What if it sells out today?' I answered.

Pat sighed and we headed off to Wigan and got lost on the way there. What should have been a ten-mile, 20-minute journey ended up taking over an hour. But we got the tree and spent a romantic evening putting it up and decorating it with tinsel and baubles.

On Christmas Eve we had planned to spend the evening together but in the afternoon Pat was invited out for a few pints with some friends. I didn't relish the thought of staying in on my own but didn't want to stop him from having fun so told him to go. And while he was out I thought it would be a good opportunity to prepare for the following day.

I was cooking a duck and a ham and all the trimmings for Christmas lunch.

While he was out I put cream rugs down on the floor

and set the table with a festive tablecloth and crackers. I stood back to admire my handiwork just as Pat clattered through the door… drunk.

He was holding a pizza and swaying. He looked at me bleary-eyed with a lopsided grin on his face.

'Happy pristmas, chrincess,' he slurred, and then dropped the pizza on the rug.

I was livid but as I stooped down to clean the rug I assured him that it was okay.

'No harm done,' I uttered through gritted teeth. I didn't want a row on Christmas Eve.

But Pat could tell by the tone of my voice I wasn't happy. We started arguing and Pat's mum, alerted by the raised voices, came to see what was happening.

She tutted when she realised how drunk her son was and scolded him.

'She's too good for you,' she said. 'Come on, Sam, you're coming back with me, you can spend Christmas Day with me.'

But I couldn't leave my husband alone on the biggest day of the year and eventually our first married row died down. Pat stumbled around and dropped more pizza before collapsing into bed.

The following morning the atmosphere inside the trailer was as frosty as the atmosphere outside. We didn't speak much when we exchanged presents. Pat had bought me a designer cardigan and perfume but we just grunted at each other when we opened them.

When Pat's cousin came in with a video camera to film the celebrations and wished us a hearty 'Merry Christmas' he took one look at our faces and turned round and went back out again.

We went to visit my mum and we went to Pat's mum's trailer and as the day wore on the iciness between us thawed.

Towards the end of the day we started speaking again. By that point I had figured that what's done is done and I didn't want my whole day spoilt.

We laugh about it now but it wasn't a great way to spend our first Christmas together.

A few days after Christmas Pat went out in the van to get some provisions from the shops. After 15 minutes I started to wonder where he was and after half an hour I began to get one of those niggling worrying feelings you get when you have an instinct that something bad has happened.

When my phone rang I jumped.

Pat's number was displayed on the screen.

'Where are you?' I answered.

'Don't panic, Princess,' he said, 'but I've had an accident.'

My heart leapt into my throat.

'What? Where? Are you hurt?' I stammered.

Pat assured me he was unhurt, he just had a bit of whiplash. The van had hit a patch of black ice and skidded off the road into a wall. The wall was demolished and the van was a write-off. I could tell he was upset – it might have been a beaten-up old van but it was Pat's livelihood. Without it he couldn't earn money.

His dad helped him tow it back to the site and he set about glumly calling the insurance company. Eventually he got a new, better van with a grabber on the back to make work easier. But all things considered, our first Christmas wasn't the ideal one I had hoped for.

# 20

# Star Appeal

Accordion music filled the trailer, but it was no gypsy party. I squeezed Pat's hand nervously; his palm was as sweaty as mine. My stomach was churning like a washing machine. I swallowed another glug of vodka and Coke to steady myself.

'Oh God, what have we done?' I muttered.

Pat was trying to act cool but I could tell he was just as tense as I was.

'What's done is done,' he said. 'It's too late to worry about it now.'

I chanced a peek outside. The windows of every other trailer on the site were lit up and flickering in time. They were all watching the same programme. It made me feel even worse. I downed another mouthful.

It was January and, months after it had been filmed, the documentary that we had agreed to take part in was finally being shown. It was the second programme in the series and we were going to be the stars of the show. As the broadcast date approached I had been getting increasingly anxious. What if they twisted my words? The people who knew we had been filmed had been asking for weeks when the show was going to be shown and that only added to my worries.

The narrator began to speak.

'For hundreds of years the traveller way of life was one of ancient traditions and simple tastes. Then their world collided with the twenty-first century.'

I groaned.

The series had been called *Big Fat Gypsy Weddings* and we had sat together and watched the previous week's programme, along with every other traveller I knew. It was big news in the community and had split opinions. Many of the younger travellers viewed it as a positive thing. It was mainly some of the more cautious, older travellers who disagreed with inviting the nation's viewers into the traveller's world. Although the show was presented as a sensational window on the UK's most secretive community, I think what it showed was only a shock to posh middle-class people.

When we were first approached to be filmed for the programme I hadn't given much thought to it. Pat was happy to agree and looked forward to seeing himself on the show. But as the months went on I started to worry. I wasn't a traveller and the show was about travellers. It just so happened that the man I fell in love with was a gypsy. I would hate for people to think that I was trying to be something I was not and I knew how some travellers felt about non-travellers and how serious they were about protecting their culture from the outside world – from influences like me, *gorgers*, as we were called. I would hate to stir up trouble for Pat and his family.

So as we sat there waiting for ourselves to appear on screen I had every reason to feel nervous.

This could backfire badly, I thought to myself. I could find myself ostracised from the community before I'd even had a chance to become part of it.

I didn't have to wait long before I was introduced on the show. I hid behind a pillow squealing as I saw myself on the telly for the first time.

'To prove her gypsy-girl credentials the bride has ordered the wedding dress to end all wedding dresses,' announced the narrator as the film showed Thelma making my dress.

I cringed. I hadn't been trying to prove myself to anyone. I just wanted a big dress! I would have ordered a big dress even if I was marrying a non-traveller. I was described as 'more of a traveller than a traveller'. The programme also made an issue of my age.

'Would you have got married so young if you weren't marrying a traveller?' the interviewer asked me. It was irrelevant. Pat was the man I wanted to be with for the rest of my life. I knew that, so there was no point waiting.

When the commercial break came on I was shaking.

Pat reassured me. 'It's great,' he soothed. 'Anyone who knows us will know and accept us. If anyone has an issue with that it is their problem, not ours.'

I went outside to get a drink. I feared the worst: curtains pulled back sharply and scowls from the other travellers. Instead I heard cheers and laughter.

'Are you watching it, Sam?' someone called over. 'It's hilarious.'

I waved and smiled, a wave of relief washing over me. At least that was one positive reaction. As the show went on I started to feel more comfortable about it.

We had no control over what was shown and how it was edited, but in the end, apart from a few gripes, we were both happy with how we had been portrayed. As the hour-long programme went on and followed the run up to our big day and the day itself, we managed to laugh about it. I saw things I'd missed on my wedding day, such as Thelma running around with her fire extinguisher and her genuine worries that the dress was going to go up in a ball of flame, and Pat's journey to the church in the truck.

After the show we went outside and spoke to Pat's family. They had loved it too. I felt a weight lift from my shoulders. If they were happy then I was happy.

That night I slept more soundly than I had for many weeks. I hadn't realised just how nervous I had been getting. And although I knew the show was watched by travellers, I didn't realise was just how popular it was with the general public. The next morning my phone was full of text messages from friends and family who had watched it and when I walked into Tesco to pick up some shopping, the lady on the till winked at me and said: 'I saw you on the telly last night.'

And that wasn't all. People stopped me in the street.

'You're the girl with the huge dress, aren't you?' they asked.

The same happened to Pat, probably even more so. We would be out and people would shout over to him. The lads at the scrapyard where he did business thought it was hilarious. And on his rounds people started to recognise him. It helped his work because when he knocked on doors people had seen him on the television and knew he was honest and hard working.

Then the interview requests started to come in. Channel 4 arranged for us to be in magazines like *Grazia* and *Now*. Newspapers wanted to speak to us. We had become gypsy celebrities and it seemed that whenever the newspapers wrote about the series, they illustrated it with our wedding photo. We became the face of *Big Fat Gypsy Weddings*.

A few days after the show we were called and asked if we would like to be interviewed on Alan Carr's chat show, *Chatty Man*.

'Why not,' nodded Pat, 'it'll be a laugh.'

We were driven down to London in a car with Thelma and the dress. There wasn't enough room to fit in all the underskirts.

I chose a gorgeous black flowing outfit to wear on the show and Pat wore his leather jacket and an Ed Hardy T-shirt. It was a long journey down but when we arrived at the studios we were treated like royalty. We were given food and drink and I got my hair and make-up done.

As the time to go on drew nearer, I started to get increasingly nervous. We had our own dressing room and I was pacing the corridor outside wondering again if we had made the right decision.

A middle-aged man in a suit wandered past. I assumed he was one of the staff there.

'You okay, love?' he asked. I obviously looked like a bag of nerves.

'I've never been on a chat show before,' I told him. 'I'm bricking myself.'

He laughed and assured me it would all be fine. And it was. Alan Carr was lovely, he came in before to make sure we were happy and we had our photo taken with him. When we walked down the staircase in the studio the audience cheered and Alan gave me and Pat a reassuring hug.

*I could get used to this*, I thought to myself.

After the show we were enjoying a drink in the green room and I saw the man I had been speaking to in the corridor again. I wanted to make the most of being with so many celebrities so I asked him where the band that had been on was as I wanted to have my photo taken with them.

'I *am* the band,' he laughed.

He was Simon Le Bon, the lead singer of Duran Duran. I hadn't even recognised him.

Then I felt a tap on my shoulder.

'Can I have a picture with you, please?' asked a woman's voice. I turned round and it was Billie Piper, the actress from *Secret Diary of a Call Girl* and *Doctor Who*.

'It should be me asking you,' I blushed. 'You're the star.'

The biggest star of the night was the R&B singer Usher. He had two burly bodyguards stationed outside his dressing room but when he walked down the corridor to enter the studio he walked past Pat and me. Pat waited for the guards to pass and then spoke to him and shook his hand.

I offered him my hand but he laughed and said: 'I don't shake ladies' hands.'

Instead he leaned over to kiss my cheek. At the last minute I turned my head so I got his lips. I know Pat understood!

It was a mad couple of months. When the royal wedding approached I was asked to model wedding dresses in the *Sun*, and the interview requests kept pouring in almost daily. We got a combined couple nickname, like Brangelina – a magazine called us Spam, which we found hilarious and which the men on the site now call Pat every time they see him.

But the star was the dress. Thelma was invited on shows all over the country and took it with her. Sadly, on a trip to a chat show in Ireland, it got damaged. Thelma had come back and the dress was being sent on separately. When it arrived back at Mum's house it was in ruins. The butterflies had been torn off, the battery packs had disappeared and most of the crystals had fallen off. I packed it away in a bag under my bed where it remained.

After the fuss about the show had died down there were some negative reactions. The series made a big deal about grabbing and I can understand why non-travellers think it is a bad idea. But it doesn't happen much and it is a well-meant ritual, not the sinister abuse some people assume it is. A lot worse goes on outside nightclubs up and down the country every Saturday night. The inference was that if a boy grabbed a girl she would then belong to him and have to marry him, which is rubbish. Pat was angry about that, too. And the show also made a big deal about fighting. Again, it is not that common and, in a way, when it does happen it is refereed and the boys stick to rules in a controlled environment. You could argue it is a better and safer way of sorting out differences between two men than drunkenly smashing bottles over each other's heads.

In some cases the programme tried to make out certain actions were traveller customs even though they were not. I was filmed when we went to pick up the page-boy suits and I covered up the price.

'Is that a gypsy custom?' the cameraman asked.

'No, it's because I don't want people to know how much they cost,' I answered.

Some travellers I spoke to thought the series was positive and that if it helped people understand more about travellers, that they are normal people just like anyone else who happen to live slightly differently, then it was a good thing. There were others, however, who felt that it exploited and sensationalised their culture. The only criticism I ever had from the traveller community was from people who left messages on the *Big Fat Gypsy Weddings* Facebook page saying that I should not have been part of the show.

# 21

## A New Life

The subject of children came up seriously in our relationship soon after Pat proposed. Although we'd talked about families before, it wasn't appropriate to start making plans until we knew we were going to get married. Only then did we know we were going to commit to each other physically. That was the traveller way and it was also my way.

We made that commitment a week after we wed. Travellers are very private about physical relationships and I would not dishonour that tradition by going into detail.

It was always a given that once we had married, the next step would be starting a family. Contraception was not an option because neither Pat nor I believed in it. I had grown up with the moral code that intimacy was sacred and was what happened when you wanted to create a life. I had told Pat that I wanted eight children, and we were both of the same opinion about starting a family, so why wait?

But as the months went by nothing happened. At the relevant time I would wait anxiously to see if there were tell-tale signs in my body, keeping my fingers crossed that the miracle of life had sparked inside me. There were a few false alarms. I'd be late and we'd both get excited.

'How do you feel this morning? Any different?' Pat would ask expectantly.

Days would pass and hopes would rise. But then, inevitably, we would have to face the disappointment of knowing that I wasn't expecting. There was never any pressure on me: Pat was happy to wait and let nature take its course but, by the first months of 2011, I felt we had been waiting too long and I began to worry that there was something wrong with my body. What if I had been damaged in some way all those years ago? I could not stand the thought that after managing to overcome the agony of the past and finally finding my happy-ever-after, the attack could rear its ugly head again and ruin everything.

I went to the doctor to see if there was anything I could do to help me conceive a child.

'Don't worry, Sam,' he reassured me after a check up. 'It's quite normal not to conceive straightaway. You need to make sure you are fit and healthy and eating a good diet and you need to be patient.'

But I still had a niggling doubt at the back of my mind.

But one day I was chatting to a friend and told her about my concerns.

'You need to take folic acid,' she told me. 'I tried to conceive for six years and it never happened. It was agony; each month was horrible. Then I heard about this dietary supplement and I started taking it and then within two months I was expecting.'

I'd heard of folic acid before. I knew that you were supposed to take it when you were carrying a child to help the baby's nervous system develop, but I had never heard of anyone taking it before as a way of boosting fertility. But I had nothing to lose so that night I asked Pat to take me to the pharmacy, which he did gladly, and after that I took a pill a day.

A few weeks later I began to notice changes in my body. I was more tired than normal and some mornings I could not face the thought of food without feeling sick. I dared not get my hopes up. It had been six months since we had begun trying and each month ended in frustration.

But Pat kept checking my symptoms on the Internet

and became convinced that it was going to be different this time.

'I know it,' he said. 'Everything it says here that should be happening is happening. And I can sense something has changed in you.'

Perhaps he meant my moods – they were becoming increasingly erratic, which Pat pointed out was another symptom. But still I refused to allow myself the luxury of hope.

'I'll give it five more days, and then I'll take a test,' I told him.

He was extra-sensitive towards me and refused to let me do anything that would jeopardise my possible condition. He wrapped his little princess in cotton wool, hoping above all else that I was carrying his child. Deep inside too I was praying for this to be the time.

The wait was agonising. Each day I woke wondering if there was any change to my condition. But the symptoms persisted and I also found my emotions going haywire over the simplest things. One night I sat watching a wildlife documentary about monkeys and when one of the female apes lost a baby, I was in floods of tears.

'I don't know what's wrong with me,' I sniffed to Pat as he gave me a comforting hug.

'I do,' he winked.

When I was ten days late I decided enough was enough. I would have to find out once and for all. Nervously I got on the bus and went into St Helens on my own to buy a test to find out whether or not I was having a baby. I was shaking at the chemist till when I handed over my money. After so many days and against my better judgement I had convinced myself by that point that Pat was right. I felt somehow different from the other times when I had been wrong. I felt changes going on in my body that I didn't quite understand.

I stuffed the test kit in my bag and hurried out of the shop. It was a 20-minute bus ride back to the site and I didn't know if I could wait that long. I was so anxious to know there and then whether my dreams had come true that I found the first public toilets I could and hurried inside where I locked myself in a cubicle and sat down to do the test. It wasn't the most comfortable place to discover something so life-changing, but at that point I didn't care. I was too impatient to wait until I was back in the comfort of my own home.

In the gloom of the loo, after doing the necessary task, I held the little white plastic stick in my trembling hand and stared at the indicator window. Every fibre of my being was praying for two blue lines. Slowly and faintly one appeared. My stomach lurched. I felt sick.

Could it be true? I waited. The packet said a positive result would be shown within minutes. The seconds ticked past agonisingly slowly.

'Please,' I whispered, 'please be positive.'

I looked at my watch. Two minutes had passed and still no second line. But still I waited. In the silence I could hear my heart beating. I dared not blink in case I missed it.

'Come on, just one more line.'

But with each passing second I could feel my dream ebb away once more. What was I going to tell Pat? He would be devastated. He was so sure this time.

The hope gave way to despair. It was not going to happen. Once again my body had played the cruellest trick on me. I blinked back tears. Five minutes had passed and still nothing. Then the anger took over. Why me? What was wrong with me?

I threw the test on the floor and crouched down on my haunches hugging my knees. Deep sobs of frustration rose in my chest. I couldn't believe that there had been so many false signs. I felt like a failure. And what if there *was* something wrong with me? Children are such a huge part of traveller life, what if I couldn't give Pat the family he wanted? Would he ditch me?

I knew in my heart that he would stick by me no

matter what, but in those despairing minutes I could feel nothing but desolation, and doubt tortured my mind.

I don't know how long I was there, wallowing in my own self-pity. I started to rehearse in my head what I was going to tell my husband, how I was going to break the news to him. I had told him that morning before he set off to work that I was going to buy a test and he had kissed me tenderly and given my tummy a knowing rub. He drove off full of hope and happiness but I was going to have to shatter those hopes and burst his bubble.

I stood up, hunched and heavy-hearted. I wiped the mascara stains from my eyelids and started to pick up my things, pulling on my coat to try and keep out the coldness I felt in my heart. As I unlocked the cubicle door I took one last glance at the plastic stick on the floor. And stopped dead. Were my eyes playing tricks?

I bent down and gingerly picked it up, holding it in front of me as if it were a live grenade. I stared, slack-jawed.

'Oh my God,' I exclaimed.

As clear as anything there were two distinct blue lines.

Anguish turned to elation in an instant. I had been wrong; the test needed more time. I was expecting!

I let out a scream. I didn't care if anyone was in there or not. The flood of excitement made my legs shake. Jumping up and down I carefully wrapped the test in some tissue paper and hurried out, fumbling in my bag for my phone as I went.

With numb fingers I punched in Pat's number and waited to hear his voice.

'Hello?' he answered.

I tried to say 'I'm expecting' but what came out was halfway between a screech and a cry. Tears were running down my cheeks as I tried to get my breath.

'Calm down, Princess,' Pat soothed. 'What's wrong?'

This time the words came.

'I did a test. It's positive. We're having a baby, you're going to be a daddy,' I gushed.

Pat cheered on the other end of the line.

'I'll meet you back at the site,' he said.

On the bus journey back I sat looking out the window dreaming about the new life that was growing inside me.

'You're going to be the most loved baby in the world,' I whispered to it.

Back at home Pat was waiting with a huge grin on his face. He hugged me and covered me in kisses.

'I'm so proud of you,' he beamed. 'You did it, babe.'

The next person I had to tell was Pat's mum. She knew we had been trying and she knew all about the problems we were having. She was overjoyed when we delivered the news. I got the same reaction from Mum.

Since I had got married and moved out we had become much closer and she promised to help me through the next eight months and give me as much guidance and help as she could. I knew with both sets of parents I had an amazing support structure around me.

Even though Pat was the one who was certain I was expecting long before I dared to believe, once it had actually happened he was in shock for a few days, and he too was as tentative as I was. We'd been let down so many times before. So a few days later I booked an appointment with my doctor. Even though modern over-the-counter tests are just as accurate as the ones performed by a GP, a tiny, niggling part of my mind refused to believe it was really true until the doctor confirmed it.

'Congratulations, Sam,' he smiled after checking the results of his test. 'You are going to be a mum.'

I skipped out of the surgery.

Once again my life was going to change. Pat and me were going to be a proper family.

I discovered over the following days that there was an etiquette involved in announcing forthcoming births in the traveller community. I couldn't tell Pat's dad or any of his uncles. I told Karen and she told Pat's father. It had to come from wife to husband and then through the men. There was no shame in expecting a baby, and everyone was genuinely pleased for us, but if I wanted to talk about ladies' things I would have to talk to either Karen or Chantelle when there weren't any males around. The men didn't get involved.

And I knew that I would have to keep my growing bump covered in front of the men – even though as the weeks went on it became obvious that I was.

Word eventually leaked out to the newspapers and my phone started to ring with reporters asking me about my plans. Was I going to have a christening? Would Thelma design the outfits?

I had already started planning. I knew if it was a boy I would call it Patrick and if it was a girl I would call it Kaiysha or Kieysha – I planned to decide on the spelling once the baby was born – or maybe Skye, my middle name. I wanted a white leather pram with pink bows for a girl and blue for a boy and I would have their name written across the top in crystals. And I would have a big christening. If it was a girl I would ask Thelma to design the dress and model it on my wedding dress with lights and mini butterflies. Of course it would have to be a scaled down version. I would never want a baby to have to carry the kind of weight in material I did on my wedding day!

Over the following weeks we started to discuss the

practicalities of raising a child in a trailer. There wouldn't be enough room in our home for a full-size cot so the baby would have to either sleep with us or in a Moses basket or a travel cot. We would only need the essentials, which was a good thing. It meant that without the space to store all the useless things lots of new parents find themselves buying, we didn't have to waste our money.

We knew that whatever happened we had plenty of aunts and uncles and family around us to help out. Pat explained that was the traveller way. The baby wouldn't have just a mum and dad, there would be a huge extended family in its life who would all be eager to look after it. Pat joked that the problem wouldn't be getting Karen to babysit, it would be getting the baby back afterwards.

We knew we would have to make sacrifices. We knew money would be tight. Just before I discovered I was expecting we had booked our first holiday together – a belated honeymoon to Marmaris in Turkey. Before that the closest we had ever come to going away together was our aborted trip to North Wales. We were looking forward to having a proper summer break by ourselves but soon released that by the time we were due to fly, although I would be allowed on the plane with a doctor's note, I would be so big, it wouldn't be enjoyable. So we cancelled the trip and saved the money to take the baby away the following year.

And now that I was expecting, I found that the early months were not easy. I suffered with terrible sickness. Most mornings the first thing I did was bolt out the door to the toilet to vomit. The smell of certain foods made my stomach turn, as did the smell of cigarettes. I had been a smoker before but I went completely off them and the smell of them on Pat made me feel ill.

My body grew and my bump became bigger and bigger. I felt heavier by the day and began to get constant back pain. The damage I had done to myself months before by wearing my dress came back to haunt me and I couldn't be on my feet for very long. I spent most days in the trailer and, if truth be told, sometimes I felt a little like a prisoner.

Pat made sure he came back from work regularly to check on me and was caring and protective. When we went shopping he would not let me carry a thing, not even a loaf of bread, and he set a timer on my phone to remind me each day to take my folic acid. I seemed to grow so much in the first two months that I made an appointment to go and see the midwife, just to check whether the due date was correct or not.

She ushered me into the examination room and began to prod around my tummy and make notes and take measurements.

As we were talking, the subject of the TV show came up. I mentioned I had recently been on television and told her the name of the show.

'*Big Fat Gypsy Weddings*?' she said. 'I saw one of them but I don't recognise you. No, the one I saw had this girl on it and she had the biggest, tackiest dress you could ever imagine.'

I decided to keep quiet.

She continued. 'Oh yes, I remember it well. It was horrendous. It had lights on it and these ridiculous mechanical butterflies. I've never seen anything so disgusting. Me and my husband were watching it and didn't know whether to laugh or cry.'

I could feel myself getting angry.

'Yes,' she finished, 'I think it was probably the worst wedding dress I have ever seen in my life. What show were you in then, love?'

'That one,' I replied through gritted teeth. 'That was my dress.'

Her face dropped and her cheeks flushed.

'Oh… err… that's just my opinion… I'm sure it was lovely though,' she stammered.

She quickly changed the subject. 'You are big,' she explained, 'but that could well just be fluid. We won't be able to tell properly until your scan.'

Then she stopped and thought for a few seconds. 'Of course there could be another possibility. Do you have twins in your family?' she asked.

As a matter of fact I did and so did Pat.

'Well, you could be carrying two babies,' she said after I told her that there were twins on both sides.

I forgot all about the abuse she had just dished out about my dress and as I left the surgery one word echoed around my head. Twins!

# 22

## Gypsy Heart

We had only just got used to the fact that we were having a baby, but that had been such wonderful news, the new bombshell that we might be having twins hardly registered.

Pat had always wanted at least two children; I knew we had some negotiating to do in the future because of my plan for eight. Maybe we would settle on five! But to possibly be having two to begin with was a good start as far as I was concerned.

'Twins?' said Pat when I told him after my appointment. 'That'd be amazing.'

I'd already started planning their special matching outfits in my head. If it was twin girls we would have an amazing christening. Thelma would be able to make matching dresses and the babies would look like two enchanted fairies covered in butterflies and twinkling lights.

I carried on growing and growing. It seemed like every week there was another item of clothing I no longer fitted into. Jeans became a problem and I started to revert back to my childhood, wearing baggy, comfortable clothes. That was one of the things I didn't enjoy about carrying a baby. You were restricted in what you could wear. The trips to Cheater Mill were not as enjoyable as they had been because there was less and less I could get into.

I developed a craving for chips and barm – a speciality of Lancashire, a bun made from hops – with gravy. At least twice a week I'd be sitting watching telly with Pat and suddenly the urge would strike me.

'Pat,' I pleaded, 'can you…'

'… go to the chippy for you?' he finished.

While I was expecting, it became a ritual. He returned each time with a steaming roll filled with chips and thick delicious gravy and I'd devour the lot and then fall asleep. The tiredness was another thing that I couldn't get used to. Most nights at seven o'clock I would be asking, 'Is it bedtime yet?'

As the weeks went by I started to think seriously about what type of upbringing our family would have and how I would raise it. There were definite advantages of living on the site. It was a secure environment. Children stayed near home and played together in and around the site but couldn't wander off because the entrance was gated. And everyone who drove on and off the camp knew there were children around and was extra careful.

If I had a boy it would be easy. In traveller life boys are afforded just as much freedom as they are in non-traveller life, probably even more so. It would be allowed to do the things all boys do and would be expected to go into the family business. The men of the family would have a big hand in guiding it and teaching it traveller ways.

If it was a girl, however, that would be a different matter. A traveller girl's life was hard and as I was living on the site I would be expected to bring our child up in traveller ways. That would mean taking her out of school and teaching her to clean and cook at a very early age to prepare her for a life as a wife, expecting her to do the housework with me. I wasn't sure that I would be happy doing that. On the one hand, I believed it would be nice to have a daughter around the home with me, but on the other an education was important in the modern world, no matter what sex you are. Pat believed children should be schooled too. I wouldn't mind if a daughter married young but some gypsy girls were taught how to clean from the age of nine and expected to do it every day. I thought that was too young. At nine all children should be carefree and allowed to play. Maybe when they get a few years older they can be expected to help around the house but I wouldn't have wanted to be a cleaner at nine and I didn't want that for any child of mine. And at the right age I would give a daughter the choice of whether she wanted to stay at school or not.

I would never intentionally disrespect the culture I married into, but I was also an individual with my own experiences and opinions and I hoped that my children grew up both as travellers and non-travellers, that I could raise them with the best parts of both cultures. I understood that my choices in the future could well raise a few eyebrows in both communities and I was not naive: I knew not everyone would be happy with some of the choices I would have to make, but I had to do what was right by my children.

And then there was the birth to plan. Traditionally, in traveller culture childbirth was a women-only affair.

I had other plans.

'If you are not there with me, I'll batter you,' I told Pat.

He explained that it was his intention to be with me every step of the way... however, there was a history of fainting at birth in his family!

I definitely wanted my mum and Pat's mum to be there with me; I realised I would have to work on Pat.

As the first months after I discovered I was expecting passed we spent evenings planning our future together.

Would we move? Would we need a bigger trailer if we had twins?

I had always hoped that one day we would be able to move to a bigger site nearby because it had wash blocks with baths and showers in. Washing facilities close to hand would make motherhood much easier but the rent on the site was much more than we were paying. There were a lot of decisions we needed to weigh up and I faced them with no small degree of trepidation. But each time I felt the nerves start to jangle when I considered my future, all I needed to do was look at my husband and be reassured that whatever happened, he would be there for me and for his family. It was bred into him, it was the way he had been brought up. Gypsy men provide for their families, that is their primary function in life. Men who can't provide for their families lose face in the community.

Since we had met it wasn't just our lives which had changed radically. Thanks to the programme we had been involved in, and thanks in no small part to my wedding dress which had achieved its own cult following, the traveller community had become more open and understood than ever before.

Of course there were critics. There were people from the traveller community who wanted to keep their lifestyle and culture secret and there were non-travellers who thought that some of the customs and traditions were wrong. But every negative was more than outweighed by a positive.

On the whole, the people who I spoke to in the community thought it was a good thing that travellers were finally getting to speak about their side of the story and to let people know about their lives. The television programmes went some way to alleviating some of the mistrust between communities. Who would have ever thought seriously before the *Gypsy Wedding* programmes that any traveller would be asked to do photo shoots and invited on to television chat shows? It would have been unheard of because of the amount of distrust between the traveller and the non-traveller communities. It is hard to believe that some of that bridge-building is thanks to my wedding dress, which was scrunched up sadly in a bag in my old room, looking tatty and worn, like some old faded film star.

I sometimes wonder what to do with it.

A lady in a shop had a suggestion recently.

'You should donate it to a museum,' she said.

It would certainly look lovely, repaired and mounted in the Victoria and Albert museum in London along with all the other historic artefacts but I'm not sure the nation is ready for that yet!

The response I had from people was amazing. One woman approached me in the street and explained that she was in a mixed-race relationship that had been badly received by people in both families. She told me that seeing Pat and me get married on the TV had given her hope. And on another occasion, after we had appeared on the Alan Carr show, a woman contacted me to say that she was a Muslim and was in a relationship with a non-Muslim man. They were both in love but had to keep their relationship secret because they were so worried what her family would say. She explained that after seeing us and how happy we were, she realised that other people's opinions were not her problem and that if a couple are strong enough, all they need is each other. She decided to tell her parents and thanked me for being the inspiration for her to go public about her love. I did not find out what happened to her but I hoped she had found the peace and acceptance that I had. I hoped she discovered, as I had, that anything is possible if you have love in your life.

Pat and I had also come from very different worlds but under the skin we were not so different. And the differences we did have certainly complemented each other.

It is a balance that will also work perfectly when we become parents. Pat will be the laid-back one, looking out and supporting while I will be the protective one, wrapping our children in cotton wool and dishing out the hugs and kisses.

Six months after we wed I found myself preparing for another big night out, my eighteenth birthday. But this time there would be no celebratory drinks. I was expecting and my condition, and the morning sickness which had progressed to morning, noon and night sickness, meant that I could hardly eat a thing. I used to think that women exaggerated the side effects of having babies but in the early months hardly a day went by when I was not sick. The sight and smell of most foods sent me scurrying to the toilet and the only things I could reasonably keep down were ginger biscuits, cheese on toast and crisps. It got to the point where most days I could not cook for Pat because the smell of food would send waves of nausea washing over me. He had to go and have his tea at his mum's. I was tired all the time and some nights would crawl into bed before seven. Pat would try his best to make me eat and look after me but most days there was nothing anyone could do to make me feel better.

On my eighteenth, however, Pat was determined to make sure I had a good birthday and took me out for a meal. I discovered I could eat steak and hungrily devoured a sirloin.

After the meal Pat pulled out a daintily wrapped box from his jacket pocket.

'Happy birthday, Princess,' he said, presenting it to me. Inside was a beautiful matching gold and diamond necklace and bracelet.

I blinked back tears of joy as I thanked him.

Weeks later we went to Whiston Hospital for our first scan and to finally discover whether we were having twins.

Nervously we looked at the screen as the sonographer passed the ultrasound machine over my bump.

'There is only one heartbeat,' she said matter-of-factly.

I didn't care that there was only one baby. I watched in awe as the features of our child appeared on the screen; its tiny arms and legs and fingers, its eyes and nose. It was perfect. Pat and I were silent. So silent that the sonographer commented.

'Most people cry,' she said.

We were simply too mesmerised to make a sound.

The lady explained that my due date would be in November 2011, almost a year to the day since we got married.

The weeks passed in a haze as we settled in to domestic bliss. In May we were invited to a party in London to hear the shortlist for the BAFTA nominations. *Big Fat*

*Gypsy Weddings* was up for an award and as the unofficial face of the show we were allowed to go to the swanky do at the headquarters of the posh bank Coutts & Co.

A lot had happened in the two years since we started our relationship. Sometimes my head swam when I thought about it. My married life with Pat, contentedly waiting to give birth to his child, seemed so different from my former life as a teenage tearaway, going off the rails at an alarming rate.

Sometimes it seemed I had lived two lives in two very different worlds. If I hadn't met Pat I dread to think where I would have ended up. He was my saviour and the traveller culture had become my safety net. When I was vulnerable it caught me and protected me. All my life I had been looking for a sense of identity, for some form of security and a place where I felt I belonged, where I wouldn't be judged on what had happened to me in the past and what I had done as a result. I found that acceptance in the traveller community. They understood me and they did not judge because they themselves have been judged all their lives.

A few months after the scan I found myself staring out the trailer window with a smile on my face. I felt a pair of arms encircle me and gently pat my growing bump.

'What you thinking, Princess?' Pat asked.

'Who'd have thought when we first met that we would end up here together with a baby on the way and a future together?' I smiled.

'I always knew,' answered Pat. 'There was only ever room in my heart for you. You were always going to be the one.'

I turned to face my husband. Lost in his eyes, I sighed.

'I think you're right,' I whispered. 'I think it was always fate that I would fall in love with my beautiful traveller boy.'

# Acknowledgements

Thank you to Pat for coming into my life and making it better. You helped me discover who I am. You are the best husband a girl could ever wish for and you have given me the most precious gift in the world – our baby.

Thank you to my family for your love and support, through the good times and the bad, and thank you to Pat's family for being amazing and accepting me unconditionally as their own.

Thank you to all my true friends and my friend Thelma Madine for making the most beautiful wedding dress I could have ever dreamed of.

Finally, thank you to Kelly Ellis and all the team at Ebury who have given me the opportunity to tell my story. And big thanks to Nick Harding for your guidance and expertise.

# About the Author

Sam Skye Lee (née Norton) was born in 1993 in Wigan, Greater Manchester. She grew up in nearby St Helen's where she continues to live with her traveller husband Patrick in a local caravan park. In 2011, Sam appeared on the hit Channel 4 series *Big Fat Gypsy Weddings*. This is her first book.